D1352480

"This is the epic story of a hugely cre̲ ces along from a Bronx which was once ̣us families to Dublin and Cork and Sli̢ ̣ to the remote Indian reservations of ___ ̣ine O'Connell Cusack dispassionately tells the story of a family that is, at once, deeply loyal to Ireland and to the United States, always alive to the endless possibilities of a life which embraces both risk and adventure."

— Damien Kiberd, broadcaster, author
and founding editor of *The Sunday Business Post*

"*Children of the Far-Flung* is more than a family history; it is the story of America and the immigrants who made it home. It is also the challenging story of Ireland and the socio-political climate that often made emigration the only option."

— Patricia Harty, co-founder
and Editor-in-Chief, *Irish America* magazine

"*Children of the Far-Flung* is a valuable memoir which intertwines a fascinating family history — the story of the Irish diaspora in the United States — with the story of Ireland over the past century. The author offers insightful perspectives from both sides of the Atlantic, and bridges the ocean with a highly readable account of human connections and family ties. If you want a sense of Irish America and its roots and ties to Ireland, Geraldine O'Connell Cusack's book is compulsory reading."

— Gerry Adams, Sinn Féin MLA, MP

"*Children of the Far-Flung* traces more than a century of the O'Connell clan, from the War of Independence, the Bronx in the Depression, Dublin in the 1960s and right up to September 11th. Uniquely, the O'Connells came back, not in the late 1990s as so many others but in the 1950s and 1960s, when everyone else was leaving. Not only did they come back but they did so with great confidence and success, culminating with Deirdre O'Connell's fantastic contribution to Irish arts via the Focus Theatre. The book sheds light on the identity crisis experienced by many Irish/Americans, their divided loyalties and ambiguous identities. But most of all, it's a celebration of mavericks, individuals and people who plough their furrow using a combination of native Irish sense of place and an Irish/American dollop of chutzpah."

— David McWilliams, economist and broadcaster

CHILDREN OF THE FAR-FLUNG

CHILDREN OF THE FAR-FLUNG

Geraldine O'Connell Cusack

The Liffey Press

Published by
The Liffey Press Ltd
Ashbrook House, 10 Main Street
Raheny, Dublin 5, Ireland
www.theliffeypress.com

A catalogue record of this book is
available from the British Library.

ISBN 1-904148-33-6

Printed in the Republic of Ireland by Colour Books Ltd.

CONTENTS

ABOUT THE AUTHOR

Geraldine O'Connell Cusack has worked as a teacher in the South Bronx in New York City, on curriculum development for a bilingual-bicultural programme with the Seminole Indian Tribe in Florida, as director of a learning facility for expatriate and local children in the Atacama Desert of northern Chile and as an Ireland Aid worker developing locally produced learning materials and Kiswahili language textbooks for Tanzanian primary schools. She now works for the Dublin City Vocational Education Committee at a community training workshop for inner-city youth.

ACKNOWLEDGEMENTS

Geraldine Ann, Aisling, Breifní, Kaniah and Tommy for their loyalty and belief, Emmett O'Connell for his enthusiasm and literary advice, Kevin and Gretta for their memories, and Damien Kiberd for reading the script and ensuring the accuracy of Irish historical facts. For use of quotations from the following interviews and publications: *The Complete Works of Stanislavsky*, The Stanislavsky Institute of London, 1951; "Dublin Women in the Arts" by Beth Ridgell, *The Irish Echo*, New York, 1980; Joe Jackson, *Hot Press*, 1984; *Dublin Focus Theatre Handbook*, 1973; Dave McKenna, *Magill*, 1982; Ulick O'Connor, Obituary of Luke Kelly, 1984; Emmett O'Connell, *Sunday Tribune*, 1986; *The Irish Times* Weekend Arts, 1968, 1969; Con Houlihan, Theatre Critic, *The Irish Press*, 1969, 1970, 1974, 1984; T. Monaghan, Co. Cavan, 1974; Nick Carter, *Magill*, 1984; Colm Toibín, *Sunday Independent*, 1985; Gabriel Byrne, *Dublin Diaspora*, 1988; Siobhan Crozier, 1990; Eileen Battersby, *The Irish Times* Weekend Arts, 1991; Katie Donovan, *The Irish Times*, 1992; Michael D. Higgins, 1997; Patricia Danaher, *Cork Examiner*, 1997; Ciara O'Dwyer, *Sunday Independent*, 1998; Con Houlihan, programme, *Gallant John Joe*, 2001; Sabina Coyne-Higgins, 2003.

FAMILY TREE OF NELLIE TAAFFE

(All dates show births, unless otherwise indicated)

Paternal: County Cork   *Maternal: County Cork*

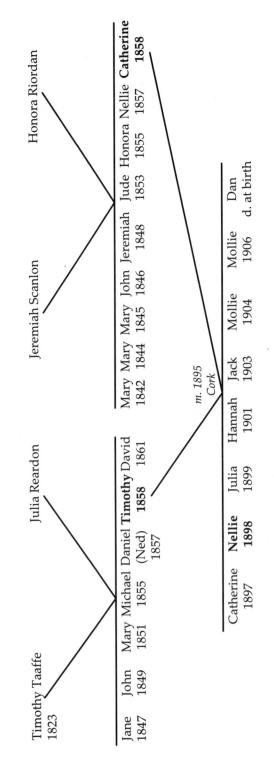

Timothy Taaffe
1823

Julia Reardon

Jane 1847 John 1849 Mary 1851 Michael 1855 Daniel (Ned) 1857 **Timothy** **1858** David 1861

Jeremiah Scanlon

Honora Riordan

Mary 1842 Mary 1844 Mary 1845 John 1846 Jeremiah 1848 Jude 1853 Honora 1855 Nellie 1857 **Catherine** **1858**

m. 1895
Cork

Catherine 1897 **Nellie** **1898** Julia 1899 Hannah 1901 Jack 1903 Mollie 1904 Mollie 1906 Dan d. at birth

FAMILY TREE OF MICHAEL JOE O'CONNELL

(All dates show births, unless otherwise indicated)

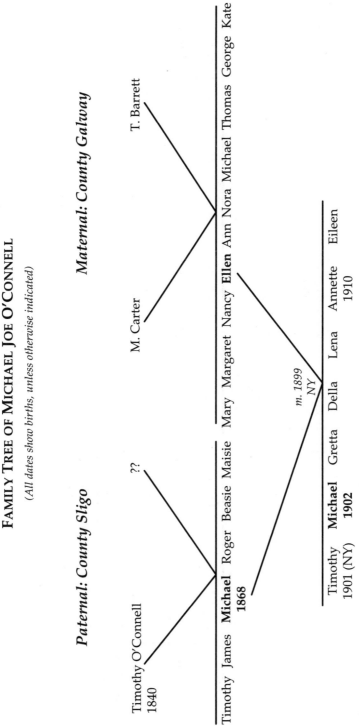

Paternal: County Sligo   *Maternal: County Galway*

Timothy O'Connell
1840

??   M. Carter   T. Barrett

Timothy   James   **Michael**   Roger   Beasie   Maisie   Mary   Margaret   Nancy   **Ellen**   Ann   Nora   Michael   Thomas   George   Kate

1868

m. 1899
NY

Timothy   **Michael**   Gretta   Della   Lena   Annette   Eileen
1901 (NY)   **1902**   1910

O'CONNELL FAMILY TREE: DESCENDANTS

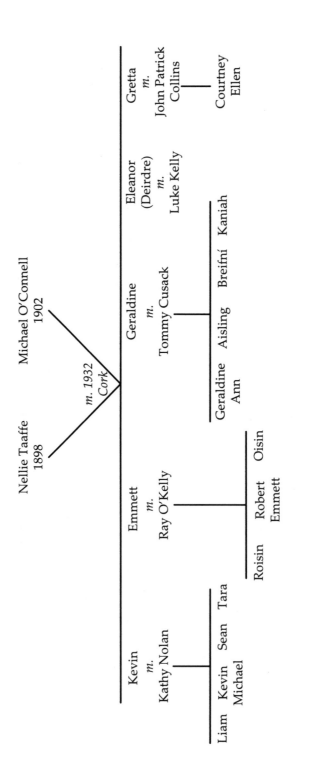

To Nellie, Michael Joe and Deirdre (our Ellie)

Chapter 1

LOVE AND HATE

CHILDREN OF THE FAR-FLUNG is what we were. Forty-eight first cousins scattered across the globe from Banteer to Brooklyn and from Sligo to Sydney. We were the South Bronx Five, born on East 135th Street between Brook and Willis Avenues. The exact street address is important. In New York City of the 1940s, each street had its own character flavoured by its ethnic mix. But ethnic is a today word — not one much in vogue in the 1940s and 50s. In those days we were all just "first generation"; the old country was Ireland, Italy, Germany, Russia or wherever — and we were all the children of the far-flung. East 135th Street was a defining point because the 135th Street Bridge crossed the Harlem River and separated Spanish East Harlem in Manhattan from the BICs. That was us — the Bronx Irish Catholics.

Dad worked in the Brooklyn Navy Yard. He got work there during the war on ships heading across the Atlantic with their cargoes of soldiers, tanks and guns. He was kept on when the war was over and he started going to Delahanty's at night to study for the civil service exams. Delahanty's was the Irishman's Harvard. It was the first step up. Off the boat, into a friendly boarding house and — next stop, Delahanty's.

As well as ship's rigger, and night-time student, and weekend security guard, our Dad was a "communist". He was that peculiar breed of "communist", though — the Irish Catholic "communist" who never missed Sunday Mass.

Michael Joe O'Connell was a tall, slim man with wiry reddish-brown hair turning grey and piercing blue eyes in a sharp, chiselled face. He cut quite a dash every Sunday morning as he strode off up 139th Street towards Willis Avenue, nattily turned out in full-length black woollen topcoat, spit and polished black leather shoes, leather gloves, white starched shirt, dark tie and all topped off with his elegant grey felt hat tipped slightly to the side. He was a proud man, our Dad, and a man of few but well-chosen words. A sidelong glance accompanied by the admonition to "stop the play acting" was enough to quell the incessant squabbling and jockeying that went on among the five of us behind his back.

And right beside him, serenely, walked Mom, the polar opposite of Dad. Mom, in her navy blue coat with the grey fur collar and sedate little pillbox hat, was small and dark and forever smiling — and she was the eternal peacemaker. "Good morning, Mollie," she would call, passing by our Aunt Mollie's house at the top of the street. And, "How are ye this morning, Mrs O?" as we turned the corner and passed another neighbour. "How's young Paddy getting on?" she would whisper to the troubled woman with the prodigal son, while Dad strode along, touching the rim of his hat in silent greeting. We were on our Sunday morning mission. We were off to Mass.

But going to Mass had nothing to do with respect for the clergy. For Dad was a fierce anti-cleric. The hierarchy, the bishops and cardinals, they were the real villains in Dad's world. It was they who had excommunicated the fighting men and women of the IRA, it was they who lived in the "bishops' palaces" back home while their faithful flock were forced to emigrate to far-off shores, it was they who lectured the poor and oppressed about the glories of the afterlife while living off the fat of the land. So Dad went to Mass in defiance of them — never in deference to them. It was his Faith, and he would be at Sunday Mass even if Lucifer himself were on the altar. And even if he managed to stay there for only fifteen minutes! How often I remember trooping out of church behind him, all five of us, mid-sermon, in silent protest at something the priest had just said. Invariably, the next day Father Dolan would arrive at our door, enquiring, "What did I say this time, Mike?"

We weren't all that sure what communist meant but we were full sure it was something shadowy and dark and a big, big secret. Why else would he and Auntie O'Keeffe, from the posh suburbs of Woodside in Queens, get into fierce arguments every time she came to visit? Our Auntie was the heart and soul of propriety. Surely she couldn't be in the wrong?

Auntie O'Keeffe had been the first of the Taaffe sisters to come to America from the north hills of Cork. Auntie was Catherine Taaffe who had married another Corkman, the pipe-smoking, gentle Dan O'Keeffe. Catherine had brought out our Mom, Nellie, who in turn brought out her younger sister, Mollie. Mollie brought Julia and their only brother, Jackie, came much later. But that's a whole other story. At the same time, first and second cousins and first and second cousins once and twice removed were on their way to Australia — that mysterious country down under. Ireland was haemorrhaging her young. That was the way of emigration. That was the way of Irish life.

CB

MOM'S OWN DAD, TIMOTHY TAAFFE, had emigrated from Ireland to Australia with his older brother, Ned, way back in 1890 when the pair of them had set off to seek their fortunes in the northern coastal gold mines of Newman. And as if that hadn't been wondrous enough, Timothy had returned to the townland of Currarague, in the village of Banteer, in the diocese of Cloyne, in the County of Cork five years later to marry Catherine Scanlon.

What kind of madness had driven a mountain farmer to traverse the globe twice, on five-month long journeys — over and back — way back then? It hadn't been the love of adventure, or place, or even for the love of a woman. Ned Taaffe had become betrothed to Catherine Scanlon before leaving for Australia and had promised to return when he had made good — like so many before him. But Ned had been a great footballer in the lands around Banteer and a favourite son into the bargain. Upon finding himself in this strange and exciting land, he set about polishing up his rising star as captain of the mine's Rugby Union. Seduced by the wonder of all things possible, any fond thoughts of Banteer and his waiting bride began to fade as his tempting new Australian saga took shape. A young woman abandoned by her sweetheart in those days faced a devastating future — alone. So Ned's younger brother by a year, Timothy Taaffe, returned home to Cork and stepped in to take his errant brother's place.

Timothy Taaffe and Catherine Scanlon were married on the 30th of July in the year 1895 in the parish of Glantane, in the County of Cork. They struggled to wrench a poor living from their scratchy mountain land. Their firstborn daughter was Catherine, then Hannah, followed soon after by Nellie, Jack, Julia and Mollie. At the age of two, baby Mollie fell into the cottage's open fire and died, and then the second Mollie was born. Twelve months later, exhausted and in need of medical help, Catherine Scanlon died in the stone cottage in Currarague. She and her stillborn infant were buried together in the lonely parish churchyard on the mountain.

Life for the young Taaffe family stumbled on, the older girls rearing the young. The ill-fated Easter Rising in Dublin in 1916 passed off unnoticed throughout much of Ireland's countryside. Not a living soul in the parish of Currarague had ever been to the capital city and it was as distant and foreign a notion as Boston or Perth. Emigrant ships to America and Australia left from the port of Queenstown and only Timothy Taaffe had ever returned to tell the tales.

But the fateful Dublin Rising brought town and country together, not through the heroism of its leaders but through the folly of perfidious Albion. For Britain had made one fatal mistake.

She had rapidly and ruthlessly put down the Dublin rebellion. It would have been nothing more than a brief footnote in the long, sad litany of Ireland's failed uprisings against British rule except for one critical thing — Britain had not been able to curb her vengeance. Not satisfied with capturing the rebel leaders, she executed them one by one, lined up against the cold and miserable walls of Dublin's Kilmainham Jail. They looked their executioners in the eyes, were blindfolded and then shot dead. The names of Padraig Pearse and his brother, Willie Pearse, Thomas Clarke, Eamonn Ceannt, James Connolly, Joseph Mary Plunkett and Sean MacDiarmada spread down country lanes and into country villages. British butchery had given birth to Ireland's War for Independence.

In the early spring of 1918, Jackie Taaffe joined the Irish Volunteers. The British general election in December of that year saw Sinn Féin win a landslide victory throughout Ireland, taking seventy-three of a total one hundred and five Westminster seats. The newly elected Sinn Féin MPs refused to recognise the legitimacy of the British Parliament. Instead, on the 21st of January 1919, they gathered in the Mansion House, Dublin, and declared this newly constituted assembly, Dáil Éireann, to be the only legitimate government of Ireland. Eamon de Valera, a surviving leader of the 1916 Rising, was elected President.

In 1919, the Irish Volunteers became the Irish Republican Army. The War for Independence had begun.

Between the years 1919 and 1921, the IRA waged a bloody guerrilla war against what they now saw as British occupying forces in Ireland: the Royal Irish Constabulary, who were the historical keepers of British law and order throughout Ireland, former British Army soldiers now known as Auxiliaries, and newly and hastily formed units known as the Black and Tans.

Recently returned from the front lines in Europe's Great War and trained to kill, the Black and Tans spread a reign of terror throughout the country, as brutal and unforgiving as that of the hated Oliver Cromwell. They were neither regular police nor regular army and they recognised no rules of conventional war. They fell between two stools, wearing the tan britches of the British soldier and the black tunic of the British constable. In response to the mayhem they left in their wake, Irish men, women and children swelled the ranks of the IRA and embarked on a guerrilla war of unspeakable ferocity. Cloaked by the dead of night, Irish volunteers ambushed British army barracks for arms and ammunition and then turned the weapons on their owners. Hillside haystacks exploded into rallies of gunfire as Black and Tan columns rolled by. Quiet country markets erupted into infernos of destruction as grenades, fired by innocent-looking farming women, found their marks. By the year of 1919, Jackie Taaffe was in action in the hills and his sister, Nellie, was ferrying him food and drink.

Nellie Scanlon, sister to Catherine Scanlon and maternal aunt to the Taaffe children, had left Currarague for New York at the same time that Timothy Taaffe had gone to Australia, almost thirty years earlier. But while Timothy had returned to Cork to marry and raise a family, Nellie Scanlon had made a permanent home in New York. She had found work and a good life, as housekeeper to a wealthy family on Fifth Avenue, and in the way of thousands of Irish female emigrants, she had never married. Hardship and despair were in Cork and her American letters had often kept a hungry wolf from their door. Now, with Ireland and her families in the throes of a savage war, it was time to do more.

Aunt Nellie sent an emigrant fare home to her niece, Catherine Taaffe, and in so doing she opened wide the floodgates to emigration once more. Catherine brought her sister, young Nellie, who brought Mollie, who brought Julia.

The Taaffe sisters went to work as practical nurses on Ward's Island, a mental institution situated on an island off Manhattan and beneath the Triborough Bridge. Ward's Island had become a haven for newly arrived young Irish. The work was hard, the pay was poor and the place itself a nightmare to reach. It was not the great American Dream. But room and board came with the job and it was a start. Delahanty's would come next.

ဢ

BACK IN THE HILLS OF NORTH CORK, Jack Taaffe had grown into a full member of the Irish Republican Army. On the evening of the 15th of June 1921, one hundred and thirty armed men gathered under the pine trees of Rathcoole Wood. There were sixty-five crack riflemen in this contingent, one of whom was Jackie Taaffe. It was the largest contingent of volunteers in Ireland. This was the notorious Millstreet Battalion of Óglaigh na h-Éireann under Commandant Paddy O'Brien, and they were lying in wait for a convoy of British auxiliaries.

The Millstreet Battalion had already put the railway line between the remote villages of Banteer and Millstreet out of action by blowing up the railway bridge at Rathcoole. The auxiliaries now had to collect their supplies at Banteer Railway Station and take them by road in their armoured vehicles back to base at Mount Leader. Commandant O'Brien and his brigade staff had been keeping a careful watch on the British movements to and from Mount Leader House and had noted that the strength of the convoy varied from between three and four armour-plated lorries with eight to ten heavily armed men in each. The lorries were covered with wire mesh to ward off bombs and grenades and were top-mounted with machine guns. They travelled approximately three hundred yards apart.

The brigade staff decided to ambush the convoy during its final supply run the following night. The men assembled in the wood under cover of darkness, where the riflemen were divided into eight sections and reinforced by volunteers armed with shotguns. All sections except one would occupy positions on the Millstreet to Banteer road and on the same side of the wood. The remaining section was to take up position north of the road.

Six eight-pound landmines were laid at intervals of one hundred and fifty yards along the stretch of roadway under attack. Three ravines leading from the wood to the road could be used in the event that withdrawal might become necessary and the sections would then be able to cover one another in retreat. The Mallow and Kanturk columns took up their positions at the eastern end of the road while the Newmarket, Millstreet and Charleville columns occupied the western end. With the mines and men all numbered, everything was ready to go.

It was 6.30 pm when the first mine, the most easterly one, exploded under the fourth and final lorry in the convoy. But the soft and boggy conditions of the road absorbed the blast and instead of blowing up the lorry, it merely cut out the engine. All sections of volunteers opened fire and were rapidly met with a barrage of return fire from the armoured vehicle. By the time the second and third lorries stopped, luck was with the British and they missed the landmines.

The leading lorry had continued its westward journey with the IRA columns on that end awaiting its approach. On hearing the rapid burst of gunfire, it swiftly reversed and ploughed into a mine. With its back wheels blown away, the auxiliaries leapt out, firing as they ran. But they were met with a powerful offensive from the waiting IRA. In a battle that raged on for an hour, machine guns blazed and bodies fell. The failure of the landmines to destroy the armoured cars combined with the force of machine guns forced the brigade to retreat. The body count was fourteen dead auxiliaries and not a single IRA casualty.

Retribution came swift and hard. Rathcoole Wood was burned to the ground and suspected volunteers were taken out, tortured and shot. Jackie Taaffe survived to fight on. Brazen and brash, his escapades became legendary around the villages of North Cork.

છ

BUT BRITAIN AND THE IRA had fought to a standstill. There would be no military solution to this eight hundred year conflict. In July of 1921, British Prime Minister Lloyd George offered a truce, and the IRA, exhausted, outnumbered and outgunned, accepted. Eamon de Valera, President of the Provisional Government of Ireland, sent his IRA Director of Intelligence, Michael Collins, to London to negotiate the peace. De Valera wanted a thirty-two-county sovereign Irish Republic. What Collins brought back was much, much less.

The Treaty of 1921 partitioned Ireland and created the twenty-six-county Irish Free State and the six-county British state of Northern Ireland. The treaty settled nothing. It opened a chasm so wide and so deep that families and villages were sundered apart between those supporting the treaty and those prepared to fight Britain to the bitter end. Now it was brother against brother and father against son.

Jackie Taaffe was now on the run from the Irish Free State Army and still fighting on the side of the anti-treaty IRA. As he sought to evade capture first by the British and later by the Free Staters, he made one dramatic escape from Mallow General Hospital dressed up as a pregnant woman. With a slight build and a height of only 5'6", he was well poised to pull it off. Jackie remained on active service right up until the IRA dumped arms in 1923. But still refusing to accept the Treaty and unable to live under it, he turned away from the land that had absorbed him since boyhood and that had asked so much. He reluctantly followed his sisters to America. Of the six surviving Taaffe children born in Ireland only one, Hannie, remained.

CзахВ

ON THE WESTERN IRISH COAST on the far western tip of Europe, a ragged coastline sheltered half deserted villages, ghostly reminders of The Great Hunger of 1847. For three consecutive years, the staple food of the Irish peasant, the potato crop, had failed and the dreaded disease of blight had left steaming black pulp rotting in the ground. The grey stone walls of Connemara crept silently over barren land, land too poor to sustain either man or beast. Hated landlords' agents torched the thatched cottages of tenants unable to meet their rents, and drove thousands of starving Irish peasants onto the roads.

The fortunate ones, those with families across the Atlantic or in Australia Far Away, found their way onto disease-ridden "coffin ships". The rocky coast of Nova Scotia or the teeming city of New York was in their sights. The less fortunate died on Irish roads, their corpses left to be picked clean by crows or buried in unmarked graves. Those either too weak to flee or too strong to concede defeat lingered on. It was from these survivors that Ellen Carter was born.

Survive they did, but they never recovered. In the intervening years between the famine and the turn of the century, counties Galway, Mayo and Sligo, on Ireland's far western shores, sleep-walked into a new century. The old landed families got on with their lives untroubled by the unrelenting poverty surrounding them. They hunted with the hounds and dined with the gentry while infants died at birth, children's bones grew twisted and bent, young mothers grew old at thirty and fathers died early from drink and despair. But there was strength in the genes and Ellen, defying all determinant factors, grew strong in body and soul.

In the year of 1891 and at the age of 18, Ellen Carter boarded the North West Railway at Eyre Square, Galway, in the heart of the City of Tribes and with her single cloth valise she set out along the mournful coast of Mayo for the port of Sligo. Her destination, like so many before her, was New York.

She wasn't long finding work in the bustling garment district of Seventh Avenue. New York City's textile industry was firmly in the grip of an East European Jewish community. They also controlled a lucrative diamond industry, which flourished side by side with their thriving clothing trade. Although the sight of Orthodox Jewish men rushing up and down the narrow, crowded streets of Manhattan with their long hair braided under little black yarmulkes and their black cloaks thundering in the city wind initially unsettled her, Ellen was made of stern stuff. This was a different land with different people. She would become one of them.

Most young Irish women of that time went into domestic service but Ellen was an oddity among her compatriots. She had a skill, a marketable skill, and she meant to make full use of it. She was a qualified seamstress. Ellen went to work as machine operator for a Seventh Avenue clothing factory and rose to the position of pattern-maker within a few short years.

Many years later, when the Bronx-born grandchildren made their first visit "home" to Sligo, the spirit that had moved Ellen in 1891 had not dimmed. Now a grand old woman of 85, long-returned to her native land, she sat regally beside the fire in the home of her daughter Gretta, clad meticulously in black, her silvery hair piled up in an elegant bun and black velvet choker around her neck. She quietly called her grandson, Emmett, to her side.

"Son," she said, "When you get back to America I'd ask you to do one small thing for me. Would you ever send me something decent to read? They keep giving me these foolish magazines and they have my head distracted." Emmett later sent her the unabridged version of *War and Peace*. She read it from cover to cover and spent many an evening after that retelling the story to Fidelma Flynn, one of her Sligo-born grandchildren.

಄

FARTHER NORTH ALONG THE WESTERN COAST, as Galway faded into Mayo and Mayo slipped into Sligo, the jagged coastline surrendered itself to blue lagoons and silver sands. The Lake Isle of Innisfree slept under the watchful eye of Benbulben. Queen Maeve's tomb rested silently at the top of Knocknarea. It was the year of 1890. Michael O'Connell had served his time, seven years as apprentice coachbuilder to the master craftsmen of the north-west and he had high hopes of winning the prized commission to build the Lord Mayor of Sligo's ceremonial coach. After all, he was the best in the trade. Everyone in the county knew it. He was an artist at his craft.

Michael O'Connell was a Catholic and Sligo was the family seat of a Protestant Anglo-Irish ascendancy. There had never been the slightest chance that he would be awarded the coveted prize. But at the age of 24, all had seemed possible. When the commission went to a far less talented but Protestant artisan, Michael read the writing on the wall. He packed his only valuable possessions, his wooden case of carpenter's tools, and took the boat to America.

It was in New York City, in the year 1895, that Ellen Carter and Michael O'Connell met. The first Irish arrivals to America after the famine had set about establishing county associations under the umbrella of The United Irish Counties and these institutions soon became a lifeline for young Irish immigrants who came after them. The Sligomen, the Galwegians, The Corkmen, The Cavanmen right down to the Antrim and Armagh men met regularly to link up with those just off the boat, suggest where work and lodgings might be found, offer tips and useful contacts and generally ease the overwhelming loneliness of this vast new world. At county dances they could meet the boys and girls from home and catch up on the news and gossip. And it was here that they would hope to meet their life partners.

Ellen and Michael met at one such county function and on the 9th of April 1899, they were married in the Church of St Paul the Apostle on East 57th Street. Ellen was a striking woman, tall and slender with her thick auburn hair swept up in a fashionable chignon. Her wedding dress was her own creation; an elegant tapestry pattern of burgundy and gold with a fitted bodice tapering in at her waist and falling gently to the floor. Michael sat proudly at her side, his ginger moustache neatly trimmed and his black frock coat and white starched collar doing him justice. Two years later, on the 3rd of January 1901, their first son, Timothy, was born an American citizen.

One would have thought that any right thinking couple would have settled down to pursuing every opening, every chance that came their way to forge a life in their adopted country. Memories of the old country were shrouded in pain, suffering, hardship, injustice, persecution, bitterness and despair. But the love/hate relationship for Ireland that haunted so many of her emigrant sons and daughters gnawed away at Michael. He hated his island for denying him his life and driving him away. Yet he craved it in spite of himself. His soul grew cold and bitter. There were no fine coaches to build among the concrete towers of Manhattan. His polished saws and anvils were brutalised on crude building sites of the Lower East Side. Elegant coaches and the shimmering waters of Sligo Bay belonged to the invader, the land usurper, the hated Saxon.

Michael's father was now well into his seventieth year and he had decisions to make. He promised the small family holding in Collooney, County Sligo, to Michael if he would return home. Land is all to an Irishman; land is never a hungry mouth, never a landlord's wrath, never having to bow the knee or tug the forelock. Land is what makes a man a man.

In 1902, Michael and Ellen, with infant Timothy, crossed the Atlantic once more and returned to an Ireland little changed since they had left more than a decade earlier. But another cruel twist of faith awaited them. In the time they had been away, Michael's younger sister, Beasie, had become engaged to a local farmer and she needed a marriage dowry. The family land was the price to be paid.

So there they were, Michael, Ellen and baby Timothy, the returned Yanks, landless and jobless, back in the land that had already dealt them so many blows. There was no going back. Too many bridges had been crossed and they just had to get on with life. So Ellen, taking the bull by the horns and the remains of their

American fortune, headed off into the neighbouring town of Balli-sodare. She had enough money to buy a leasehold of ten acres on the estate of landlord Major O'Hare.

Our Dad, Michael Joe, was the second-born son of Ellen and Michael in their new homestead at Glenagola. *Gleann na Gualithe* — the glen on the shoulder of the mountain. Gretta, Della, An-nette, Lena and Eileen followed.

The O'Connell homestead stood on a hillside in the shadow of the Ox Mountains. Little time was spared to meditating on the wonders of nature. Wild strawberries and blackberries, abundant in autumn, were harvested and potted, and the jams made by Ellen and the girls were sold to estates as far north as Donegal and Leitrim. Two cows gave rich milk and a fine flock of hens content-edly laid for home and market. The small, rocky holding was nur-tured with care and gave plentiful supplies of potatoes, carrots, parsnips and onions. Apples were the preserve of the Major's or-chards but, like the rabbits of the fields and the pike of the streams, they found their way to the O'Connell table courtesy of Timothy and Michael Joe.

Though life was clearly better for the native Irish in the far north of Sligo than in the mountains of County Cork, Major O'Hare was never far from mind. On the first day of every month, his land agent, immaculately turned out in riding jacket, starched collar, britches and boots would gallop up the country lane. Dust and steam rose from the heaving flanks of his magnificent mount. Pulling up on the dirt track in front of the cottage, he would roar:

"Sir's rent, if you please!"

He, the landlord's agent, was more hated than the landlord himself because he was one of their own. Without dismounting, he would accept the offered rent money and without a tip of the hat or a nod of the head he was off — to the next unfortunate fam-ily in his bind.

The bush fires of the War for Independence had spread north as well as south and Michael Joe was a young man of fifteen. Manhood came early in those days; schooldays were a luxury for the rich and well-born. Poaching rabbits had to be abandoned. It was now time to defend the homestead at Glenagola from marauding bands of Black and Tans. Young Annette's post on the breast of the hill approaching the cottage gave clear vision of torchlight attacks on isolated homesteads and the time needed to raise an alarm. Michael Joe could then spring into action. His father's intricately carved farm cart, strategically positioned behind the house, gave cover.

One frosty night in the winter of 1919, that cart was set ablaze and tongues of flames licked the starlit sky. Minutes later, two Black and Tans lay wounded on the bend of the Ballisodare Road. Timothy and Michael Joe became hunted men and the fortunes of the O'Connell family changed once more. Crops were systematically burned and the chicken coop looted. The land agent never failed to appear on the appointed day each month and the rent was always met, but now it was the skilled dressmaker's hands and not the carpenter's tools that made the difference. Hard times had come rattling at the O'Connell door.

◌ঙ

THE END OF IRELAND'S WAR FOR INDEPENDENCE brought with it The Treaty of 1921. It was a bitter pill for the ordinary people of Ireland to swallow.

Sligo was predominately on the Free State side. It was a complex society into which Michael Joe O'Connell had been born. A large landed class of Anglo-Irish dated back to the early English settlements of the 1500s, that pivotal time in Irish history when Irish landowners had been driven from their lands and large plantations of English and Scottish settlers had replaced them. Those plantations had left many a mark on the native people.

The estates of those powerful Anglo-Irish dynasties had spread an influence far beyond their land boundaries. For centuries, so many of the ordinary townspeople had been dependent on the Big House of the estate for their living. Cooks and chambermaids, gardeners and groundsmen, carriage builders and drivers, herdsmen and gamekeepers, they and all their descendants had held a grudging regard and often a blood relationship with the landlord. Birth on the wrong side of the blanket was not uncommon. Although denied recognition by the lord, recognition by the village offered elevated status, dubious though it may have been. So the Treaty of 1921, demanding sides to be taken by all, drove an even deeper wedge between an already fractured community. Divided loyalties had begun to raise their heads.

The Free State forces in the border counties engaged their new enemy, the IRA, with a newfound zeal. Former comrades-in-arms went out to settle old scores and ended up brutally annihilating one another. The O'Connell family soon found itself split apart.

Timothy, the first and American-born son, supported the Treaty and joined the Irish Free State Army. "Better half a loaf than none at all," he reasoned. Michael Joe was anti-Treaty and remained staunchly on the side of the IRA. "It was not for a partitioned land that we have all fought," he argued. Nonetheless, his loyalty to Irish republicanism never extended to its leadership. It was from Dad that we first learned the meaning of the strange world "quisling". He always used it when referring to "Dev". Dad would then carry on: "The seething outrage of our betrayed people could be heaped on the head of Michael Collins instead." To Michael Joe O'Connell, Eamon de Valera became truly the most devious, the most cunning traitor of them all.

With the restoration of law and order to the new nation, an unarmed police force, known as the Garda Síochána, was established. Timothy O'Connell became one of its first recruits. He was among the contingent of new Irish gardaí who stood at attention as Britain's Union Jack came down from Dublin Castle for the last time and the Tricolour of the Irish Free State rose in its place.

But truth to tell, Timothy's heart was never in it. He was part of a force that was policing a troubled land. The passions of Ireland's bitter Civil War simmered on below a thin veneer of peace. Past loyalties were transferred to the new political realities but mistrust and suspicion reigned. Divided families and communities struggled to put the past to rest while unreconstructed rebels carried on their fight for sovereignty along the new and noxious northern border.

The Irish Free State Army and the Garda Síochána were the defenders of the new state and Timothy was part of that. Sooner or later he would be called upon to hunt down his own brother, Michael Joe. It was a reality too hideous to conceive. So Timothy took his American passport and departed for America. And with that, another wave of O'Connell emigration had begun.

On his arrival in America, Timothy O'Connell had no problem joining New York City's Finest. As an American citizen and a former Civic Guard, he was pushing an open door. He soon discovered that his early life in the hills of Ballisodare stood him in good stead and he rapidly rose to the rank of Sergeant in New York City's Mounted Police. For years to come, he proudly led the annual St Patrick's Day Parade up Fifth Avenue. Carrying the Stars and Stripes of the United States, he would turn his head sharply to face the imposing edifice of St Patrick's Cathedral and take a dignified salute from one of America's most influential religious leaders, New York's Francis Cardinal Spellman.

Back in the hills of county Sligo, the new Irish Free State held nothing for his younger brother, Michael Joe. He would never give his allegiance to a partitioned state, a state that had cut off six of its counties and handed them over to Britain. He existed on the fringes of life, running in the shadows and fighting for a hopeless cause. Ireland was partitioned. The six counties were part of the United Kingdom. All around him were war-weary people ground down by poverty. His only family support, his young sister, Annette, had been sent off to join a convent in Texas. It was her parents' attempt to keep her out of harm's way, a safe port in a never-ending storm.

Michael Joe could take the boat to England as so many of his neighbours were doing. But to seek refuge in the arms of the oppressor would be an act of unthinkable treachery. So he set his sights elsewhere.

During the 1920s, Sligo was a busy seaport with freighters from North and South America using its harbour as a transfer point to Britain. Michael Joe had only hazy images of those far-off lands but he was mortally tired of fighting and running. The new Ireland was a poor substitute for his shattered dreams. He was a young man who wanted a future. He would find it in a distant place called Uruguay.

The very name conjured up exotic visions with unimaginable possibilities. He signed onto a vessel shipping out for its capital city, Montevideo. He planned to jump ship in port and make a new life in South America in the gallant tradition of another Sligoman, Ambrose O'Higgins, the father of Chile's honoured liberator, Barnardo O'Higgins.

But fate had other plans in store. In 1928, the very week that Michael was due to ship out to Uruguay, an emigration visa to America arrived in the post. Timothy, as an American citizen, had been able to sponsor his application for resident alien status.

CзахB

MICHAEL JOE'S ENTRY INTO AMERICA was not nearly as neat as Timothy's. He was the typical Irish "greenhorn". He had left formal education at an early age and demolition was not a highly regarded American skill. So when Ward's Island beckoned, he answered. And it was on Ward's Island that Michael Joe O'Connell met Nellie Taaffe.

Nellie and her sisters, Catherine, Mollie and Julia were all what was known as "practical nurses". That is to say, they had no formal medical training. They had begun their working lives at the bottom of the nursing ladder. They changed bedpans and washed bed linen. But they were smart and they were ambitious and they soon found their way to Delahanty's night school. It was the thing to do if you were an Irish immigrant.

From bedpans they progressed to practical nurse status, preparing medications and keeping detailed medical charts. Catherine eventually became a fully qualified registered nurse, as did her first cousins from back home in County Cork, Abbie and Mary Scanlon.

But Michael Joe was never very happy on the island, as he was not cut out for the caring professions. His temperament was highly strung and he was impatient. He had come from a turbulent past and the regular routines of hospital life unnerved and unsettled him. But while the glittering lights of New York City in the Roaring Twenties were electrifying the world, a Great Depression was looming on the horizon. Wall Street suddenly crashed in 1929, and with queues of homeless men and women lining the streets and flooding emergency soup kitchens, Michael Joe and Nellie clung to their jobs at Ward's Island. Now was not the time to start building castles in the sky.

A match between Nellie Taaffe and Michael Joe O'Connell would seem to defy all understanding. Nellie was, to all outward appearances, the most gentle of souls; soft-spoken, kind and generous to a fault, with never a harsh word for anyone. But beneath that gentle exterior there was a steely resolve. Few in America knew anything about her early days with Cumann na mBan in the hills of north Cork — or of her steady and regular remittances to her father back home. Those faithful letters had kept the small family landholding going during all the years of her absence.

Ward's Island, New York
20th Feb. 1929

My dearest Father,

We are all fine here in New York thank God and hoping this letter finds you the same. Myself and Catherine are still at Ward's Island and with God's help will be here for many years to come. How are you keeping — I hope well. And how is Hannie? Tell her to rite and tell me all the news. I am sending you these dollars for the spring planting — they are pasted to the back of the letter for safekeeping. Hoping you stay well and with God's help I will rite again this day next month.

Your loving daughter,

Nellie

Timothy Taaffe had never been the best of managers and the emigration of all but one of his children had taken the heart out of him. His farm was in constant danger of being lost to drink or unscrupulous land grabbers. So despite the uncertainties of the time and the ever-present threat of losing her job, Nellie's regular monthly letters helped to keep the salivating packs at bay.

ଔ

IRELAND, ITS TORTURED PAST and its compromised present was no longer in the cards for Michael Joe. He had joined the American Federation of Labour and at night he soaked up American history, politics and economics at Delahanty's. "I never stepped inside the door of the schoolhouse," he would remind us as we laboured over our sums on the big round kitchen table in the Bronx. We knew exactly what was coming next. "I only heard the schoolmaster as I was passing by." An exaggeration, to be sure, but the deprivation of any real schooling beyond the primary class had left him with an unquenchable thirst for knowledge. He had been a reluctant farmer, a disillusioned revolutionary and a miscast caregiver and he had chosen none of these. Life had got in the way of all his dreams but at the age of 28 he was wresting control. He would not relinquish it without a fight.

Nellie was also happy and content in New York. Her eldest sister Catherine had married Dan O'Keeffe, another Corkman, and had settled down to raising a family in the thriving Irish-American section of Woodside, Queens. Mollie was keeping company with an exotic young seaman of Irish-Portuguese descent by the name of John Ferreira and Julia was engaged to be married to a dashing, if somewhat "unreliable" New Yorker. Cousins Abbie and Mary Scanlon were working their way up the nursing ladder and another cousin, Sister Mary Pius was with the Sisters of Charity at a very posh girl's college in New Jersey. Then there was the extended family of Scanlons, Riordans and Conlons and second and third cousins once and twice removed, all living within a stone's throw of one another in Queens.

Franklin D. Roosevelt would soon be elected President of the United States and begin to put the American nation back to work by pouring millions of dollars into public works schemes. So life was definitely looking up. The one discordant note in an otherwise harmonious glow was with the notorious Taaffe brother, Jack.

Unlike Michael Joe, who had put his turbulent past behind him and looked to his future in America, Jack had never been able to settle in his new home. He was an inveterate charmer, the life and soul of any party, while at the same time the proverbial fish out of water, because County Cork was never far from his mind.

As the years passed and life under Ireland's Free State Government stumbled into what was called normalcy, Jackie yearned to return home. But on the death of his father, Timothy Taaffe, and in defiance of local custom, the family farm was bequeathed not to him, the only son, but to Nellie.

It is here that history begins to repeat itself, for it is a foolish man or woman who would deny the vagaries of the human heart. Michael Joe was a single-minded and determined man. One could never imagine him stepping back in time — not even for love. But against all the odds, Michael Joe succumbed. Nellie Taaffe and Michael Joe O'Connell left New York City in late summer of 1932 aboard the Cunard Line's *S.S. Mauretania* bound for Queenstown, now the newly rechristened port of Cobh in County Cork. They were married in the Church of St John in Mallow Town on the 21st day of August of the same year. Nellie and Michael Joe were home to do what their parents had done a generation before them; they were the returned emigrants, ready and anxious to begin a new life on the family farm. And if life had continued along this chartered course, we, the South Bronx Five, would have been born in Curraragh. Clearly, fate had something else in mind.

Maybe they had been away too long. In those days, once an emigrant left Ireland's shores, he or she was never expected to re-turn. Visits back home were out of the question. There were new lives to be built and families to rear. America was the land of op-portunity but there was no gold to be found on her streets. Suc-cess came only by the sweat of the brow and it was not to be thrown away on man's foolish dreams. The Irish emigrant was expected to make good in his new country but never forget the old one. He had a solemn duty to remember the folks at home. But he was not meant to go home. The eagerly awaited American letter and the American parcel were evidence of that.

So this unexpected and wholly unwelcome turn of events created turmoil within the Taaffe family and within the local com-munity as well. Jackie Taaffe was the stuff of which legends are made. He was the daring, swashbuckling hero of the Kilbroney Massacre. He was the trickster who had conned the British and Irish Free State armies as well. He was the returning hero, certainly not the returning emigrant. By virtue of this, he was fully entitled to inherit the family farm.

The Taaffe family had a long and eminent history going back to the Austro-Hungarian Empire. Their most prominent ancestor, Nicolas Taaffe, had been a viceroy in the Court of King James. He had spent his adult life in Hungary and had married a princess in the Emperor's court. In return for his loyal service to the Crown, Nicolas had been granted title to land in what was later to become County Cork. The descendants of Nicolas eventually fell upon hard times and most of the land was squandered or lost, but the inherited genes remained strong. The distinctive almond-shaped dark eyes and jet black hair passed down from generation to generation and lived on in Jackie and Nellie and to a lesser degree in their other siblings.

"Who is this blackguard, O'Connell?" demanded the crusty old farmers hunched over their pints in Healy's pub in Banteer. "I'll tell you who — a blow-in, a thieving interloper from the west." And the stinging gossip on the tongues of all those meeting along McCarthy's Bridge was all the same. Never mind that the land was Nellie's and not Michael's. Never mind that Michael Joe had given his young life to the same cause as Jackie, and against the same enemy. Never mind that he had fought on the same side as Jack in the Civil War. "All politics are local," as they say in Ireland, and Michael Joe was certainly not that.

Neither did he have the easy charm of Jackie Taaffe. He was tall of build and fair of face, with an unruly thatch of ginger hair and his eyes of topaz blue held you with a steady gaze. His taciturn and unyielding manner made few friends in this tightly knit community in the hills.

Against such a background, Nellie and Michael Joe and a new life in Currarague never had a chance. The whispering campaign grew apace with the resurgence of prosperity on the long-neglected land. New rumours took wings and spread beyond the parish. This was a stronghold of anti-Treaty forces and a depository of long memories. "His brother joined the Civic Guards — protectors of a dominion state. Not sovereignty! Dominion! What does that tell you about his loyalties?" Damnation by association is what it was.

Too proud to endure the torment of local jealousies, Michael Joe prevailed upon Nellie to relinquish the land. Within a short two years of their expectant homecoming, another dream had come to a crushing end. It was the emigrant's passage once more and this time, it would be twenty long years before either one would set foot again on Irish soil.

႙

Chapter 2

THE MELTING POT

URING THE DYING DAYS OF THE 1920S, and just before the onset of the Great Depression, an ambitious plan had been mooted in New York City, a plan to demolish three square blocks of crumbling tenements and seedy night spots between 48th and 51st Streets to make way for a new Metropolitan Opera House. But the Wall Street Crash had intervened.

In 1931, on that original site, millionaire John D. Rockefeller Jr inaugurated the biggest private building enterprise America had ever seen. Between 1931 and 1939, four thousand New Yorkers went to work on what was to become a spectacular hub for the radio broadcasting industry, Rockefeller Center. Here was a testament to America's belief in America, a labyrinth of spectacular underground shopping malls that connected a bewildering maze of towering office buildings. Radio City Music Hall opened in 1932 with the imposing General Electric Building rising 70 storeys into the New York sky. From the entrance on Fifth Avenue, a majestic promenade of swaying trees and seasonal plants led to an outdoor plaza, an oasis of peace amidst the austerity of urban concrete and steel. In winter, the plaza was transformed into an outdoor ice rink, with skaters swirling and shoppers bustling beneath the most famous Christmas tree in the world.

Michael Joe and Nellie had returned to a fragile America but Michael Joe, nonetheless, found work as an ice-maker on the

Rockefeller Center skating rink. Kevin, their first child, was born in the Bronx, in 1934.

But Kevin had entered the world as Raymond Gregory. There was no good reason for this choice; no family history and no historical link. Nellie just liked the names. So Raymond he was, until Michael Joe appeared at the hospital and, scandalised at this Americanisation of his first-born, Raymond Gregory became Kevin after the young Irish patriot, Kevin Barry. Taking no chances with the next child, the name was chosen before the birth. A year later Emmett made his entrance and was called after the martyred patriot, Robert Emmet. There then followed in quick succession, Geraldine (that's me), after the mighty Geraldines of County Kildare; Eleanor, after Nellie, Grandmother Ellen Carter, and Eleanor Roosevelt; and Gretta, after Michael's sister.

Eleanor Roosevelt? What was an icon of the American political establishment doing in the middle of that Irish mix? The wife of Franklin Delano Roosevelt was a strong social reformer and a loyal defender of the working class and for Michael Joe, that was more than enough to merit a place in the roll call of Taaffe-O'Connell women.

The O'Connell family, having grown rapidly, moved from just over the bridge on 135th Street to a more spacious apartment with three bedrooms on East 139th Street.

East 139th Street was a world unto itself. Brook Avenue lay to the east of this crowded city street and it took its name from the early days of the Dutch colonial settlement, when New York had been New Amsterdam and the Bronx had been rich, green farmland. To the west lay Willis Avenue, the district's commercial hub. But between those two official land boundaries existed three distinct divisions known only to those who lived there.

The bottom of the block, where we lived, had an assortment of redbrick and stone-faced apartment buildings, which, at the turn of the century, had been elegant residences for the rising middle class. But with the Great Depression of 1929, all vestiges of wealth had disappeared. In its wake came a new immigrant wave, the DiMaggios from Sicily, O'Herrs from Germany, the Goldbergs from Poland, the Repkos from Czechoslovakia and Rio and his family — from Brazil. And eventually, there came the O'Keeffes, the O'Connells, the O'Malleys, the Crowleys and the Mahoneys from Ireland. It was a stew of national identities bubbling away in peaceful coexistence. But the main ingredient was unmistakably Irish.

We lived at Number 488, which means that there were nearly 500 houses on that street alone. The local public elementary school, PS 9, adjoined our apartment house and it became the dividing point between us and the next section of the block.

That section, the middle of the block, was strictly Italian territory and much more "with it" than our poor patch. They had the candy store and the Italian market, and their young men were already beginning to sport scandalous white socks, pink shirts, greased-back hair and pegged pants. Our parents issued daily warnings to stay well away from such corrupting influences. But they needn't have worried. We, the backward Irish *"greenhorns"*, would have been beaten out with sticks and stones had we dared to invade their protected turf. *West Side Story* in the making is what it was.

The top end of the block was the domain of those gracious brownstones we used to see on *The Cosby Show* on TV. It was the place of dreams. From the bottom to the top of the block; although it was but a few hundred metres in space, it was one giant step on the road to success.

The other road to immigrant success was through the civil service system, and Delahanty's Night School was always the route to get there. Ice-making was now a year-round job but Michael Joe needed something more. He had a rapidly growing family and with labour relations in the workplace at a low ebb, trouble was definitely brewing.

The ice-makers at Rockefeller Center were agitating for a negotiated wage increase but as the workforce had not yet become fully unionised, their negotiating power remained weak. Following several weeks of labour unrest and with continual threats of strike action in the air, management called for a meeting with the workers. Word spread rapidly that a new pay deal was on the agenda.

A sharp-talking, cocky and confident site boss took the floor. He drew a clear picture for the assembled workers on the realities of private enterprise. "It is," he said, "like a table with four legs. Each of the legs is of equal value and together they must balance the table. At one end we have the investor, the owner of the enterprise, and at his side sits management, those who run the operation. On the other side of the table we have the workers and at their side sit the labour unions. Those are the four legs. But unfortunately for all of us, one side is unbalancing the other. Labour is upsetting the balance and if we don't rebalance the table, the whole enterprise will collapse."

He then prompted the assembly to rise and applaud the entrance of the great man himself, Mr John D. Rockefeller Jr. John D., as he was known to the men, would proceed to outline the solution to the conflict.

The assembled multitude rose to their feet, clapping and cheering, but not yet aware of the conditions on offer for settlement. A sprinkling of men remained firmly in their seats and among them was Michael Joe.

Company detectives, known as "dicks", spread out around the hall, zooming in on the stone-faced recalcitrants who sat among them. "What's your name, buddy?" one spat out to Michael Joe. There was no reaction and no answer. "What's this guy's name?" he hissed to the man standing beside Michael Joe's chair. There was still no answer. Then he turned to the fellow standing on the other side of Michael. "What's your name, buddy?" "Paddy Cullen," came the reply. "And him, what's his name?" pointing to Michael Joe. Again, there was no answer. Then came the bombshell: "Paddy Cullen, you're fired."

Then the "dick" returned to the first of the standing silent men. "So now, buddy, what's this guy's name?" That man had five children. "Michael O'Connell" came the muffled reply. And with that, Michael Joe O'Connell was fired.

ଓ

THE BROOKLYN NAVY YARD was the centre of shipbuilding on America's East Coast and the workforce was heavily weighted in the direction of Italians and Italian-Americans. But through tenacity and grit, Michael Joe landed a job in the middle of blue collar Little Italy. For an Irishman not long off the boat, it was a real coup.

Having just learned a very hard lesson from John D. Rockefeller Jr, Michael Joe immediately joined the labour union. It was led by an enigmatic and volatile fellow immigrant from County Kerry, Michael J. Quill. Quill would later move on to lead the powerful and much-maligned New York City Transit Workers' Union, and he became Michael Joe's mentor. The energy and convictions that Michael had expended at home against Ireland's oppressor, Britain, were now levelled against the oppressors of the working man. Ship's rigger was Michael Joe's job; union organiser was his new passion.

All through our childhood, Dad was a two- and sometimes a three-job man. He worked in the Brooklyn Navy Yard by day and then he left to do his second shift for Wells Fargo Security at night. He had left a very promising career with the much larger and more prestigious company of Pinkerton Security and transferred to Wells Fargo when, while doing an assignment for his evening class in American History, he had discovered some very unpalatable facts about Pinkerton's dark and ugly past — facts connected with a secret Irish-American society known as the Molly Maguires.

Famed in American legend and song, the Molly Maguires had been an Irish-American labour movement that had started in the late 1850s. As a result of the Great Hunger in Ireland in 1847, millions of Irish peasants had landed on American shores, and in the great cities along her eastern coast, this wave of bedraggled and bereft Irish immigrants had been greeted with signs loudly proclaiming, "No Irish Need Apply". So thousands had travelled on and settled in the teeming mining towns of Pennsylvania, towns bounded by the Blue Ridge Mountains to the south and Susquahanna Valley to the north. There, the hazards and cruelties of mining life had roared an uncertain welcome to the otherwise despised and rejected Irish immigrants.

The history of the Molly Maguires is shrouded in myth and propaganda. They have been described as everything from ruthless murderers and brutal terrorists to courageous men who were struggling to support their families and improve working conditions for the exploited miners. One's interpretation of whether they were heroes or devils depends largely on where one's loyalties might lie. For Dad, it was no contest. The Molly Maguires were right up alongside the great labour leaders in Ireland's past, the courageous James Connolly and the indomitable James Larkin.

At that time in the history of American labour relations, unscrupulous mine owners wielded almost total control over the lives of their workers. They employed highly paid site bosses to enforce brutal working conditions and private police forces to crush any simmering unrest. A complicit printed press waged relentless campaigns of vilification against all potential union organisers and demonised the Molly Maguires with vivid stories of drunkenness, thievery and wholesale thuggery.

Nonetheless, historical evidence shows that the Molly Maguires managed to spread a reign of terror across Pennsylvania's mining country that lasted for more than twenty years. Sabotage, destruction, murder and mayhem became their stock in trade as they fought to break the iron grip that the mine owners held over their workers. Unfortunately, the Mollys were fighting a purely tactical war. They never developed a clearly thought-out strategy that could carry the movement forward towards a focused set of long-term goals.

Their final undoing began in 1873 when Franklin B. Gowen, mine owner and proprietor of the Reading Pennsylvania Railroad, decided to crush the Molly Maguires, once and for all. He was determined to succeed, whether it took six months or six years. His long-term goal was crystal clear. It was to wrest total control over the production and distribution of coal. The treacherous and meddling Molly Maguires were upsetting his bold, enterprising plan.

To accomplish the goal of absolute corporate control, Gowen engaged the services of Pinkerton Security and a newly recruited detective named James McParland. McParland's mission was just as clear as Gowen's goal: run down the leaders of the Molly Maguires and remain in the field until every "cut-throat" paid for his villainous deeds with his own life.

McParland acquitted himself well. Within eighteen months of his recruitment by Pinkerton, he had infiltrated the inner core of the Mollys. A privately funded police force arrested nineteen members of the organisation on evidence provided by this privately funded investigator. Nineteen men were tried by corporate prosecution attorneys and found guilty of murder. They walked to their deaths on the state gallows, and the Molly Maguires were no more.

Although the Molly Maguires were subsequently consigned to legend and the pages of history, they had paved the way for others to join in the fight for workers' rights. In 1890, the most powerful force ever to emerge within the American labour movement was born. It was none other than the radical United Mine Workers Union. Our Dad tucked that new bit of information securely away in his head and moved on to work for Wells Fargo.

 C8

WE LOVED THE WELLS FARGO JOB because Dad was night watchman at an ice cream plant and once a week, on Saturday night, he would come home early from work with one of the fringe benefits of the job — gallons of sumptuous ice cream and satchels of round, sugar-coated malted milk balls.

In preparation for his arrival, Mom would call us in from the street at five o'clock for our baths. Our hair would be washed and

dressed and elaborate ribbons and bows were tied into our cork-
screw curls. Then, with freshly ironed dresses on the girls and
clean shirts and pants on the boys, the five of us would parade
down to the Brook Avenue subway station to meet Dad on his
way home from work. We felt like little princes and princesses
living in the South Bronx.

As he emerged from the subway, our eyes would be riveted on
the brown paper sacks that he carried in his arms. Everyone in the
neighbourhood knew our routine because most of them were part
of it. Old Mr Goldberg, standing sentry on the steps of Number
488 with his brass-tipped cane and oval-rimmed glasses, would
flash us a curious glance as we trooped by. That wise old owl
knew that all the kids in apartment building number 488 would
be having a special ice cream treat that night.

The entryway to 488 was grandly called the "lobby" and it was
the gathering place for all our street games. In summer, we would
collect there in our swimsuits to watch and wait as the Crowley
boys quietly crept up on the fire hydrant outside our door. Then an
iron wrench that had been carefully hidden beneath one of their tee
shirts was suddenly whipped out, the hydrant cap swiftly un-
screwed and hundreds of gallons of city water blasted out onto the
hot, steamy street. With a flat piece of plywood held in front of the
gushing gallons, these boys could manage to raise a spray clear
across from one side of the street to the other. Some of the boys
were better at it than others. Jimmy Crowley had refined the art of
the "Johnny Pump" to such a fine degree that the water rose forty
feet into the air and came down as soft as the morning rain.

This emancipated "Johnny Pump" always brought dozens of
kids running and screaming from all directions. We leapt and
danced and shouted at the top of our lungs as the icy needles
pricked our sunburnt skins. Our make-shift shower, with its bit-
ing cold spray, drenched passers-by and passing cars alike and
raged on until New York's Finest invariably arrived in patrol cars

to turn it off, all to our taunts of "Brass buttons, blue coat, couldn't catch a nanny goat!"

With that bit of diversion finished for the moment, the gang would turn its attention to either Kick-the-Can or Ring-a-Levio. The first game required each kid to find two Coca-Cola cans and, laying them on their sides, stamp one foot into each so that the cans resembled tight-fitting horseshoes. This procedure demanded a high level of street cred. The stamp had to be strong enough to force the sides of the can up and over the sole of the shoe and well positioned enough so that the can could cling on securely. With one can attached to each shoe, the contestants would clatter off down the middle of the street, called the gutter, with each kid kicking another can as far as he could. The kid who reached the farthest point in the gutter without losing his can-shoes in the process was declared the winner.

Ring-a-Levio was a horse of a different colour altogether, a team sport that couldn't just be dreamed up at a moment's notice. No, this game required careful team selection and team planning and could engage up to twenty or thirty kids at a time. The bossiest and pushiest of the kids on the block were usually the captains of the two teams — and that meant the Mahoneys and the Crowleys. Jimmy Crowley was a few years older than the rest of us and he had his favourite players; Kevin always got on his team and Emmett sometimes made the cut, but not always because he was small and skinny. But he was fast, so that helped. The rest of the gang would be chosen according to age, size and sex until everyone available was accounted for. The teams would then claim their territory; base one was the Jewish Synagogue across from our house and base two was our front stoop. The public schoolyard was always home base.

With team selection and land claims completed, the captains would take up positions in front of the opposing side. When the signal was given, they would race out to confront each other in the middle of the gutter. The object of the confrontation was to get past the other captain without being tagged. They then had to race on towards their own teams, who were in jail, and release one of them by tagging and shouting at the top of their voices, "Ring-a-Levio". Then all four members had to head for "Home" to the roars of their supporters, and reach base untagged before being declared free. The freed members then joined the expanding confrontation in the middle of the gutter, and this went on until all of one team or the other had been freed. As the game progressed, there could be twenty screaming and hysterical kids running in all directions, dodging passing cars and leapfrogging fallen heroes. Anyone tagged had to return to jail. The game could go on for hours and sometimes it ran into days. We were a persistent lot with little else to do on long, hot summer nights.

All of life was lived out on the sidewalks of New York. On sweltering summer nights with temperatures reaching ninety degrees Fahrenheit and above, bed mattresses were hauled out onto our tenement fire escapes in the hope of catching an elusive night breeze. Then with the dawning of morning's first light, and with all the dads gone off to work, our moms would set about shepherding squads of children off the streets and on to the city parks. Fortified with shopping bags filled with bologna sandwiches and a sugar-based coloured water drink called Kool-Aid, we would set off on a three-mile hike to Randall's Island.

Randall's was an oasis of tranquillity that sat beneath the Triborough Bridge. In order to get there, we had to cross a series of pedestrian paths that zig-zagged through the middle of this traffic-clogged motorway. Cars, buses and trucks whizzed past us on their way to their destinations in the Bronx, Manhattan or Queens. We trundled along, sandwiched between streams of flowing traffic, with dust and fumes blowing in our eyes and the very structure of this mighty bridge swaying under us. For us kids, this was wicked fun. We skipped over metal cracks in the footways and scared ourselves silly by peering down into the vast depths of white water that crashed beneath our feet. And at the end of the trek, we entered a parkland of green grass, leafy shade and properly patrolled water showers. For our moms, it was a blissful release from the pressure-cooker of our hot city streets.

The winter season brought with it a very different assortment of city sports. The snow blizzards of the 1950s are a thing of legend and old-time New Yorkers tell of city streets completely closed off to traffic for weeks at a time. Snow fell faster than it could be cleared away. As city sidewalks were cleared and mountains of snow were shovelled onto roadways, these tightly packed snow banks swiftly turned into walls of ice. For gangs of kids thrashing around in this avalanche of snow, the appearance of ice walls was the signal for "war" to begin.

Snowball wars were deadly serious affairs. Captains and teams had to be carefully chosen and sturdy snow forts constructed. Then an arsenal of approved ammunition had to be laid on long before hostilities could commence. Since we had no military hospital, ice that was packed inside the snowballs could cost you the game.

When our gloves became sopping wet from all the snow-packing and snow-throwing, a truce could be called. Then the gangs could retreat to the "lobby" to peel off their sodden coats, leggings and gloves and lay them on the steaming radiators to dry. There was never a thought given to going home to change or warm up. Once inside your house, chances were you would be kept in — so it was better to suffer the stinging cold and chilling wet than miss out on all the fun.

CR

WE WERE SERIOUSLY INTO WAR GAMES on our block. The United States had recently emerged from a devastating war in Europe and the even worse war in the Pacific. Victory in Japan Day had been celebrated with a monster street party that had begun in the public school playground but soon spilled out onto the adjoining streets. The mellow music from Glenn Miller and his band swept out over cheering crowds. "Don't sit under the apple tree with anyone else but me" poured out over mounted loudspeakers and was followed by "Sweet Rose of San Antone", "Deep in the Heart of Texas" and "Pennsylvania 65000".

But as day turned into night and the singing and dancing crowds swelled, life-sized effigies of Germany's Adolf Hitler and Japan's General Tojo were tied to street lampposts and set alight. These grotesque images swayed and danced in the night sky, blazing, crackling and spitting like drunken spirits.

It was the frightening expression of so many mixed emotions, a manic mingling of joy and sorrow, love and hate, the rapture of being on the winning side in a horrific war and the agony of losing so many young lives in the struggle. It was the pain and confusion of ruptured cultures and divided loyalties, with old Mr Goldberg and gentle Mrs O'Herr peering out timidly from behind twisted curtains at the milling, cheering, intoxicated crowds.

The street kids had their own generals and soldiers and we even had our own street slogans; the East 139th Street slogan went like this: "Whistle while you work, Hitler is a jerk, Mussolini is a meanie and the Japs are worse."

Returning GIs who had served in France or Germany or Japan were our greatest of heroes. If you happened to be lucky enough to have an older brother who was a GI, well that made you a hero too. We, the O'Connell clan, weren't fortunate enough to be in that elevated class but we did have an older cousin, John O'Keeffe, who had landed on Omaha Beach in Normandy and had returned home unharmed. Mom always said it was our prayers bombarding heaven that had brought him safely home. So we, too, basked in his reflected glory.

Our upstairs neighbour, Joey DiMaggio, no relation of the famous Joe DiMaggio, made us sick to death boasting about his hero brother. One day, he appeared on the street with a small box, a souvenir that brother Tony had brought home from Japan. Inside the small square box was a bed of cotton wool and sticking out of the wool was a bright yellow finger — the colour of a war enemy. As we gathered round and stared into the box with morbid fascination, the finger moved. We dispersed, screaming, in all directions while Joey doubled over laughing on the sidewalk. He had painted his own finger yellow and pushed it up into the centre of the box.

Our apartment was on the ground floor of 488 and our next-door neighbours were an elderly German couple called the O'Herrs. A strange appellation for a German family, one might rightly think. They owned a German bakery and our Mom was very fond of Mrs O'Herr. Every evening, Mrs O'Herr would knock on our door and deliver a piece of homemade apple strudel or a loaf of German rye bread. It wasn't until I was nearly an adult that I discovered the true derivation of the O'Herr surname.

The letterboxes in the lobby of our building carried the names of all the tenants, and our neighbour's name was actually Herr Oscar Schmidt. Since Mom unintentionally turned every name she ever came across into an Irish one, the Oscar Schmidts became the O'Herrs. They never corrected us, true friends as they were.

We had another haughty neighbour that we called Mr Paperhanger. This gentleman had a certain air of importance about himself and he had even engraved his occupation onto his letterbox. We couldn't pronounce his name, and we weren't particularly fond of him either. So he certainly didn't warrant an Irish name. We settled on Mr Paperhanger. Then we had the O'Malleys who lived in the apartment just above us whose sons carried the marvellous names of Jeremiah, Jacob and Moses. How their only sister had become a very pedestrian-sounding Nancy is anyone's guess.

ଔ

WE ALL BEGAN OUR SCHOOL DAYS in the school adjoining our apartment house, Public School 9. Everyone considered it a very old-fashioned kind of building, even back then. Most modern school houses had a large auditorium that could be used for school functions and neighbourhood events but our two-storey building had a cavernous empty arena on the ground floor that was used for indoor basketball and softball games and a shared space for administration offices. All the classrooms were on the second floor.

But what we lacked in modern architectural design, we more than made up for with ingenuity. All the classrooms had walls built on tracks. Those walls could slide back and magically transform a dozen or so individual classrooms into one large assembly hall. School Assembly was the focal point of every day.

At 8.45 sharp every morning, the school bell rang, the walls rolled back and three thumping chords from Mrs Shapiro's Steinway piano heralded the entrance of the PS 9 school colour guard. Dressed in navy blue trousers, white shirts and red ties, two eighth-grade boys flanked the proud flag bearers as they marched with heads held high through the student assembly. With the Stars and Stripes securely installed on stage and with hands on hearts and all eyes fixed firmly on Old Glory, in unison we began to recite:

> *"I pledge allegiance to the flag*
> *Of The United States of America*
> *And to the republic for which it stands*
> *One nation, under God,*
> *Indivisible*
> *With liberty and justice for all."*

There we stood, scrubbed, polished and erect, stumbling over strange words in what was, for some of us, a strange tongue. But we learned those words off by heart and I doubt if any of us ever forgot them. New Americans in the making, that's who we were.

At PS 9, all the teachers were Jewish and most of the students were Catholic. The Jewish teachers couldn't pronounce our names and they couldn't understand our English, probably because we spoke a form of pidgin English. All of our parents spoke with Irish brogues and European accents.

For Irish immigrants, this meant a heavily accented English with a generous smattering of old Irish expressions thrown in, *mar dheá*? So the O'Keeffes and O'Connells, the Mahoneys and Crowleys, the O'Donnells and the O'Malleys all grew up using a flourish of old Irishisms, convoluted sentence structures, criminally distorted English words and all the while thinking we were speaking perfect English.

When we wanted to ask the meaning of something, we would say, "What's that inaidov?" not knowing that there were three words in that expression and it really meant "in aid of" — or, what is that for? The teacher was an *amadán* or even an *oinseach*, for not knowing that. We didn't know that there was a distinction between male and female fools; she just wasn't too bright, anyway you said it. And I was only after telling her what I was on about!

It really was *exstroidinry*. When I wanted to use that word in a story, I couldn't find it in the *dicshinaree*. The *amadán* of a teacher didn't know I wanted to say extraordinary and I was only gobsmacked when I discovered that you put two words together and made something that meant "out of the ordinary" out of it. It just didn't sound anything like that at home.

Confusion was compounded when we started to add bits of Yiddish, like *"Oy vey"*, to our conversations and then threw in a little Italian like *"Mamma mia"*. When I left our neighbourhood of the South Bronx and entered high school in downtown Manhattan, I suddenly discovered that not everyone spoke like me. But all the other immigrant students had their own peculiarities, so English Composition became the most important subject on every school timetable.

The first teacher I ever had was called Mrs Jaaffe. It was probably spelt differently, but my Mom's maiden name had been Taaffe, so Mrs Jaaffe it was. I hated her. She was big and fat and forever cross. And she could never understand what I was trying to say.

For punishment, she would make me sit on the floor under her desk, with her big, fat legs kicking and pushing me the whole time. She must have been demented, now that I think of it, to do a thing like that. But I never said anything, probably because teachers were always right. And if I was being punished, well, I must have done something wrong. I just couldn't figure out how to change it.

Every Tuesday was Release Time Instructions day. At the beginning of every school year, parents of children who attended the city's public schools were invited to complete the pink Release Time slips provided by the Department of Education and take them to their church, chapel or synagogue to be stamped. The completed forms were then returned to the school principal.

At 1.45 pm on the designated day, the school bell rang and all those who had applied for Release Time gathered up their coats and books and filed out to the waiting buses. They were off to prepare for First Holy Communion, or Confirmation, or Bar Mitzvah or Bible Study. I adored Tuesdays. They were heaven-sent, a blessed release from the *extra ordinary* teaching style of our demented Mrs Jaaffe.

But Guggenheim Dental Clinic day was a true nightmare. Every student had an opportunity to have his cavities filled or his decaying teeth pulled out, free of charge, provided his parents had signed the "card". One Monday afternoon when my turn arrived, I climbed aboard the school bus and headed off to a destination unknown, confident in the belief that I would return home with a dazzling new smile.

The clinic was a huge, frightening building downtown, a place where we, from the South Bronx, never went. I must have been very small at the time because the doctors in their white coats looked like monsters. They were all very big and they were all women. They clamped my mouth open so wide that I wanted to cry. But instead, I squeezed my eyes shut tight and frantically prayed, "Please God, don't let them hurt me!" When they had finally finished poking and drilling and spraying into my mouth, I looked up to see big black numbers tattooed across their arms.

Those lady doctors scared the living daylights out of me. They didn't speak English, at least not my kind of English, and I had heard whispers that they were refugees from Hitler's concentration camps. They had come to America after the war and were practicing their dental skills on us public school kids. Whoever or whatever they were, they took the nerves out of my two front teeth and eventually my teeth turned black. That put paid to my dazzling smile. Years later, when I was *flaithiúlach*, that is to say old enough to pay for the work myself, I had to have them filed down and capped to make them presentable to the public.

Jewish people were always very big players in our world. The Synagogue was just opposite our house and it was a source of everlasting mystery and intrigue. Every Saturday evening, at around 5.00 pm, a crowd of kids would line up on the bottom step of the Synagogue and wait for the old rabbi to come out. His humped back, his long black flowing robes, his bushy grey beard and his black yarmulke petrified us. We were transfixed. With hearts thumping and palms sweating, we waited for the crooked finger to point to one of us. He never spoke. With a slight nod of his grizzly head and an even slighter indication from his trembling hand, he chose. Then the appointed one would get up and silently follow this sinister figure into his den. He would shuffle through the building, pointing to one light switch after another, which the appointee would turn off, little by little plunging the spooky Synagogue into total darkness. Saturday was the Sabbath and no work, not even the switching on or off of the lights, could be done. So the Christian child would have to oblige.

At the final light switch, the rabbi would pull back a heavy velvet curtain and lift a dark cloth from the edge of a table. Under the cloth were two copper pennies. Payment for the *goyim*.

Then one day, as we sat huddled on the stoop waiting for the beck and call, our brother Emmett suddenly announced that we were going on strike. We were being reared on strikes. Dad always had the latest news. People were out on the streets, striking and picketing for their rights. Either the garbage men had just come off strike, or longshoremen were going on strike, or the transit workers were already on strike. So now, it was our turn to strike for a better wage.

"Two pennies is not enough," Emmett told us. "The rabbi can't turn the lights off himself so he needs us. And we should be getting a nickel at least." So there we sat, rooted to the spot, as the rabbi beckoned in vain. Finally, Emmett rose and approached the puzzled old man. The rest of us sat staring straight ahead, not daring to look in case we were struck down dead on the spot.

Quite unexpectedly, the *"bould"* Emmett disappeared into the darkness, only to emerge five minutes later, back into the light, with fantastic tales of skulls and bones and horrible smells, and more grist for the ever-turning South Bronx mill. And with a shiny new nickel in his fist.

All our daily shopping was done at Harry the Jew's, a thriving grocery store on Brook Avenue owned by a man called Harry Salit. Mom and Harry were great friends and we bought everything "on tick". We were forever running down to Harry's for a bottle of milk or a loaf of bread. Mom made her own soda bread and brown bread, so sliced soft white Wonder Bread, enriched, was a sometime treat. When we didn't have jam, it was bread and butter with sugar sprinkled on top. The slate was always cleared with Dad's pay packet at the end of the week.

Then there was the curtain store, a real Aladdin's Cave with satins and laces and all the finery that was needed for christenings and First Holy Communions. It was owned by another Jew. There were no politically correct language police in those days, so we called everyone by what they were: The Jew, The Chinaman, The Polack, The Czech and if we couldn't pronounce the name or the nationality, then the place he or she came from would have to do. For instance, when a new boy came onto the block from Brazil, bearing an unrecognisable and unpronounceable name, he was immediately nicknamed "Rio" and he became one of our best friends.

One of the "Polacks" in our neighbourhood was Mr Levy who had come from Warsaw. He ran the Chinese laundry, even though he was clearly not Chinese. We spent endless hours on dark winter nights, listening to him telling stories about his life before the war. We could see the cold, dark streets of Warsaw, its shuttered windows and its rolling fog, as Mr Levy rambled on and white starched shirts trailed down around his shoulders from trestles attached to the ceiling. The shirts draped around him like creatures from another place. Mr Levy's crackling voice entranced us and we were slowly hypnotised as we watched him switch rhythmically from one heavy iron to the next, resting the iron that had gone cold onto a flat metal plate that sat over red hot coals. Then he would remove a freshly heated one from the plate and carry on. Baskets of wet shirts sat at his feet and sweat rolled down his face, even on the frostiest of nights.

C3

AT THE AGE OF TWELVE, Kevin was the first of us to "go to work". Our janitor was an American Czech named Mike Repko. But we called him our "super" — short for house superintendent. We were beguiled by words, rolling new ones around on our tongues and spitting them out in the most inappropriate of places. We loved the sound of some and hated others. "Janitor" was just plain nasty. So we called him our "super".

Mike had been in the war and had met a real Czech named Susie while he was fighting overseas. He married Susie in Europe and brought her home as a war bride. Susie's mother followed shortly after that, and we all called her "Grandma", probably because so few of us had grandmas of our own living in New York. They were all back in "the old country". Mike, Susie, Grandma and the three children all lived together in one of the apartments in Number 488.

The reason that Mike was our "super" was that an apartment went with the job and Mike could work another job at the same time. Everyone we knew was double-jobbing. After all, this was America, and in America this is what new Americans did.

Every evening, Mike would patrol the houses under his care and check the electric bulbs in the ceilings in the halls and on the stairwells. He had a long wooden pole with a nifty little attachment on the end. When he found a bulb that had blown, he would unscrew it with the light pole and replace it with a new one. Kevin became his assistant, carrying the supply of new bulbs in one hand and the discarded ones in the other. Eventually, he was promoted to other duties, like sweeping down the stairs and emptying the dumbwaiter.

This dumbwaiter was a spectacular device and it was great fun into the bargain. Every apartment had a door in the kitchen wall that opened up into an empty cavity. Inside the cavity, a contraption made of ropes and pulley ran up and down the side walls. When you pulled on the ropes, a wooden platform appeared at your door. You loaded your garbage onto the platform and sent it whizzing down to the basement where the "super" was waiting to receive it.

This exercise took place at 6.00 pm every evening and Kevin became the dumbwaiter specialist. That is, until one day a dead cat appeared on the platform. That ended Kevin's fascination with the dumbwaiter and he went back to changing light bulbs.

Mike was a great friend of the family and known by all the tenants to be smart and very ambitious. His wife, Susie, was a tremendous worker and an even better cook. After putting in a few years as house "super" of Number 488, and working at several other part-time jobs, he managed to buy a small delicatessen situated right beside the entrance to Brook Avenue subway station. The family moved into an apartment behind the deli and the kitchen of the apartment became the catering centre. Grandma, with her ponderous form swathed in a big navy-blue overall and with her grey hair covered in a cotton babushka, would sit with a huge basin of steaming hot potatoes balanced between her knees, peeling and slicing and listening contentedly to Verdi or Mozart on an old phonograph machine.

At the age of nine, I became baby Susie's babyminder and Grandma's kitchen assistant. The baby-minding was the easy part. I would wheel Susie around to our apartment and Mom would feed and change her while the rest of us played with her. There were always dozens of school friends in our house, either watching Mom in the kitchen making soda bread and apple tart, and waiting to lick the sweet spoon from the mixing bowl when she had finished, or waiting for a bit of the sweet *"crackleen"* off the top of her roast pork. Some would be poring over homework assignments while others listened to the adventures of Roy Rogers and Trigger on the radio. Baby Susie was propped up on pillows in the middle of the floor, taking it all in.

Being Grandma's assistant was a little more difficult than that bit of diversion. She spoke no English at all and she had hands like leather. They were desensitised. She felt nothing. Piping hot potatoes flew through her fingers like magic. My tender fingers could not keep up, so I was soon relegated to mixing sugar, oil and vinegar into the German potato salad and delivering it to my brother, Kevin, who had been promoted to counter service in the delicatessen.

Every Saturday evening, I paraded home in triumph with the fruits of my week's labour: two dollars for Mom and a large bottle of Coca-Cola and an apple pie for the rest of us. I felt ten feet high.

Mike and Susie Repko were not long for the Bronx. They had much bigger plans. Young Michael was taken for voice lessons when he was only nine or ten years of age and was singing opera in the back of the deli while I was peeling potatoes. Eventually, they sold the deli and moved to an idyllic mountain resort in up-state New York, called Germantown. They bought a roadside diner there and, when I was fourteen and had my legal working papers, I spent a summer working as a waitress under the watchful eye of Grandma. I returned home at the end of the summer chuffed with myself, as I spread out hankies stuffed with nickels, dimes and quarters on my bedspread. My sisters Ellie and Gretta gasped in amazement at the fortune I had amassed. They were my tips for the season.

The Repkos weren't the only ones on the move. We too made the great leap forward in the year 1950. Dad had been preparing to take the New York City Civil Service exams for years. He studied at Delahanty's Night School a few nights a week, while working at the Brooklyn Navy Yard by day and at the security job on weekends. When he finally felt confident enough to sit the exam, he passed on the first go. His assignment was to a post in the Department of Correction, a euphemism for the notorious Riker's Island Prison situated in the middle of the East River. Dad was never a warder; correction was not his style. He was appointed as chief supervisor in the prison inmates' mailroom.

‎ಣ

WITH A NEW AND BETTER JOB under Dad's belt, Mom and he took courage in their hands and bought a three-storey brownstone house in the middle of the block. It was a small difference of a few hundred yards up the street, but it was a huge step up the ladder to success. It would be our own home on a proper piece of land. We would no longer be tenants. It was all that every Irish family ever wanted.

We moved house in the dead of winter, in the middle of a snowstorm, by snow sled. We didn't own a car, nobody we knew did. Anyway, there was nothing we couldn't do for ourselves. So with the help of the DiMaggio's ice truck and all the gang's sleds pooled together, we pulled our furniture and all the rest of our bits and pieces up the middle of the snow-packed street, having a whale of a time jumping on and off the beds and sofas and in and out of the snowdrifts.

Dad led the way inside the ice-truck with Old Mr DiMaggio. We never knew his first name, and anyway, it would have been impolite to use it even if we had known it. Our elders were always addressed by their title and surname only. So he was Old Mr DiMaggio from Sicily, as opposed to his son, Mr DiMaggio from the Bronx. His dark, handlebar moustache was a familiar sight in the neighbourhood as he plied the city streets with his blocks of ice. Meticulously dressed in black trousers and vest and a white cotton shirt, he would deliver this ice to all the apartment tenants twice a week, chipping off a block just big enough to fit into the top compartment of our iceboxes. Then he would throw a canvas bag over his shoulders and haul the block onto his back with a pair of huge iron tongs. He was a great old warrior, Old Mr DiMaggio, climbing five and six flights of stairs with his heavy load hundreds of times a day. And he ploughed this long furrow well into his seventies.

Old Mr DiMaggio lived in one of the brownstones up the block, where we were now heading. Occasionally, when they were in season, Old Mr DiMaggio would arrive with a pocketful of sweet dates from his back garden. They were dry and pulpy and we didn't like the strange texture. But we knew our manners, we were reared to be polite to our elders, so we thanked him profusely and tried to discover what Sicilians could possibly find so great about this weird concoction.

The young DiMaggios lived two flights up from us in Number 488 and they had a magic pot that sat bubbling on their stove from dawn to dusk. Every so often, Mrs DiMaggio would lift the pot lid and throw in a few more over-ripe tomatoes, sprinkle in a teaspoon of foul-smelling white powder or pour on a few more drops of olive oil. And the pot would carry on simmering and spitting throughout the day. By six o'clock in the evening, the tangy smells from the DiMaggio apartment filled the hallways and stairwells and the family sat down to evening meal. Spaghetti was being served.

Pickled pigs' crubeens, tenderloin and cabbage and baked hake with turnips and carrots were all very well, but we, the O'Connell clan, hankered after a taste of the foreign. So one day, after yielding to our insistent pleadings, Mom prevailed on Mrs DiMaggio to teach her how to make the red sauce. We were sick with excitement as we tripped over one another to get at the magic pot now bubbling on our stove and sample the spicy foreign flavours therein.

That night we gathered around the kitchen table as usual and waited expectantly as Mom ladled out piping hot noodles and an angry red sauce onto Dad's plate. Puzzled by the glutinous glob shimmering around on the plate in front of him, Dad called over to Mom as she stood with arms folded over her flowered apron, watching solemnly with her back to the stove. "Say, Nellie," he asked, not sure how to begin, "Do I get any potatoes with this?"

Refrigerators came into use in middle America soon after the war. But we weren't real Americans. We were Irish, or German, or Italian-Americans, we had names like Patrick, Mary, Roberto, Alphonse and Klaus and we lived in crowded apartments with iceboxes and on crowded streets with numbers.

Americans were called Sally, Dick and Jane, like the children in our school readers. They had pet dogs called Spot and soft, white kittens called Puff. They lived in white clapboard houses on leafy streets called Elm Drive. I often daydreamed about such places as I sat in the health station park, surrounded by sleeping babies and squealing toddlers, reading about exotic-sounding towns like Savannah and Williamsburg. As I conjured up romantic images of gracious ladies sipping mint juleps under a spreading magnolia tree, I wondered again and again what it would feel like to be an American.

ဢ

Chapter 3

GREENHORNS AND NARROWBACKS

NUMBER 445 ON EAST 139TH STREET in the South Bronx opened up a window to a new world for all of us. Suddenly, the cramped quarters of apartment living gave way to a three-storey house with a backyard. Now we were "on the land".

Dad took to vegetable gardening in a big way. During the long summer evenings, he religiously tended his rows of sturdy tomato plants, his neatly banked ridges of Long Island potatoes and his beds of beetroot and carrots. He would end the night's work by clipping and pruning our single apple tree, then stand back and admire the fruits of his labour. Everything had to be orderly and tidy. When everything had been finished to his complete satisfaction, Mom would call him in for his tea.

One evening he came home from work with a rusty old statue of an Elizabethan couple, whom he quickly christened "Romeo and Juliet". He had rescued it from one of the security job's dumpsters. He painstakingly sanded down the rust, re-pointed the bits of iron that were damaged and painted the romantic figures subtle tones of silver and deep green. Romeo and Juliet took pride of place under the budding apple tree.

A circular cement path ran around the sides of the backyard and in winter we poured water onto it and watched it freeze. Hey, Presto! We had our very own ice-skating rink. Who needed John D. Rockefeller now? We didn't have ice skates but the makeshift coke-can running shoes came in very handy.

Three concrete steps led down from street level to an enclosed square in front of our house, which everyone called the *"airey-way"*. To this day, I do not know what the English word for that space was meant to be. Maybe it was area way or something like that. It certainly wasn't cool and breezy, so it couldn't have been an "airy" way. In fact, on a hot summer's day, with New York's temperatures soaring to ninety degrees Fahrenheit and above, the aireyway was more like a blazing furnace.

A black cast-iron gate led from the aireyway into a small space under the stoop, the stoop being the twelve steps from street level that led up to the front door proper. But we were never allowed to use that door. We went in downstairs, behind the iron gate. There was a storage space under the stoop which Dad called the "Dead Man's Box". He had a penchant for rechristening everybody and everything he came into contact with; so President Truman became "Short Pants Harry", Josef Stalin was "Iron Joe" and the garbage collectors were "Sherman's Army" leaving a trail of destruction behind as they tipped overflowing garbage cans into their trucks.

Number 445 was no palace when we first moved into it. It needed a whole lot of doing up. So for the first few years, the girls all slept on a pullout bed in the sitting room, beside Mom and Dad's small box bedroom, and the boys were upstairs on the first floor to the back. A big country-style kitchen was at the back of the house and it opened out into the backyard.

We had a large round wooden table in the kitchen which we all sat around for dinner each night. Mom served the meal and then sat down opposite Dad, between Ellie and Gretta. Emmett was on one side of Dad and Kevin on the other. I was somewhere in the middle. Emmett was positioned in this way so that he was directly in front of the cutlery drawer that was built into the lower rim of the table.

Emmett had been born with a murmur in his heart, so he was always considered to be "delicate", needing extra attention and many, many vegetables. Unfortunately, Emmett hated peas, carrots, turnips and parsnips, all of which made up a big part of our everyday diet. So when Dad's head was turned to another giggling insubordinate in his company, with his fork raised and the admonition, "Your ear is very close to me" ringing out over the table, the vegetables went into the cutlery drawer. This was a nightly occurrence. We knew that they knew but everyone carried on as though no one knew. It was part of a continuing mania that passed as normal family life.

Dad liked to think he ran the house with military precision. We had rules for everything. For instance, money was never to be mentioned. To ask what somebody did for a living, or God forbid, how much that somebody got for that living, was to plumb the very depths of vulgarity. Other than the ice cream job, we never even knew exactly what Dad did for a living until we were adults. Money was no concern of the young!

One rule that was particularly irksome forbade us to go into the kitchen while Mom and Dad were having their evening tea. That ritual took place every evening at 8.00 pm when they sat at the kitchen table, talking and talking and telling secrets we could have no part of. All we could do was stare in at them mournfully through the glass door.

Sunday evenings were special nights because we got to sit up and listen to "Dorothy Hayden's Irish Memories" on the radio with Mom and Dad. It was during one of those Sunday night sessions that we discovered an amazing secret about Mom's past. She had been a "Charleston" dancing queen during the heydays of the Roaring Twenties. Out came photos of our Mom, that diligent Bronx housewife, all decked out in a beaded flapper dress and strapped sandals with her black bobbed hair rippling in soft waves down the sides of her face. She was utterly beautiful, a goddess, a film star. We couldn't stop staring — at her, then the photos, then back at Mom. We were bewitched!

Dad laughed proudly as he took us up on the floor, one by one, and whirled us around to the strains of Mickey Carton playing

"The Rose of Mooncoin". And Mom tut-tutted contentedly, shifting piles of sewing on her lap as she watched her young daughters learning to dance — not the Charleston, but the old-time waltz.

The basement of our house held a huge pot-bellied furnace that had to be fed with shovels of coal every few hours to keep the water hot and the house warm. At 9.00 pm every evening, Dad would go down to "bank the fire", that is, to cover the flames with *clinkers* and slack so that the fire would smoulder but not go out overnight.

When the fire had burned itself out, the burned coals were emptied from the bottom of the furnace and shovelled into an empty coal bucket to cool. Then, in rotation, we had the job of picking out the clinkers. These were the coals that were burned clear through and couldn't be used again. When you hit a clinker off another piece of coal, it made a clinking noise. Hence, the new word, clinkers, was born.

The basement floor was made of concrete and it was always cold and dusty. So Dad decided to paint it, to make it a little more hygienic for our night-time chores. And we were warned not to walk on the floor until it was completely dry. Dad went down to the basement shortly after the warning had been imparted, and found a trail of footprints imprinted all across his newly painted floor. Being a man of few words, he called the five of us together into the kitchen, lined us up in front of him, and began an inquisition.

"Why did you do it?" he questioned, one after the other, to the alarmed and tearful responses of "I didn't do it. Honest. I didn't do it." Then the circle began again, and again, with the same interrogation and increasing levels of distress. "One of you has to have done it. Which of you is lying?" Oh, my God. Someone was about to be caught out and, in our house, lying was the ultimate sin. "Tell the truth and shame the devil." That's the simple motto that we O'Connells were to live by.

But, as luck would have it, the doorbell rang and in walked Auntie O'Keeffe. Our Saviour. Our Emancipator. Dad had been right on the verge of asking to see the soles of our shoes, to expose the craven coward that was harbouring amongst us. And it was Me. Oh, the mortal terror of it all! Punishment could be endured, but never the shame! To be exposed in front of everyone as a liar! Would I ever have recovered? Not in a million lifetimes.

෫

THE THREE GIRLS REMAINED ROOMLESS until one day the ceiling fell in and crashed down on top of the bed we had just vacated. I think that experience scared the life out of Mom and Dad, more so than ourselves. Had we been in bed, we would have all been killed. But the silver lining appeared when we were given the back room upstairs, all to ourselves, right beside the boys' room. And then the fun really began.

We were always cautioned to put the latch on the door after we entered the room for bed, probably because we had paying guests on the top level. These were our "roomers". But Dad had invented an ingenious little device for safety and escape — just in case the house caught fire in the middle of the night and we were all locked in. He had sawed out a section of the wall between the two bedrooms just big enough to put a hand through and reach the latch on the adjoining bedroom. So, if some untoward and dreadful event did occur in the middle of the night, we could re-lease the boys or they could release us, and we could all hurl our-selves out of harm's way and certain disaster.

The trouble was, once Mom had checked that we were all safely tucked in, and had descended the stairs, all hell broke loose. Latches were released and the tearing in and out of each other's bedrooms would begin against a background of hollering and screaming that would waken the dead. Then the warnings would start to emanate from downstairs. "Cut out that racket or I'm com-ing up! I'm not telling ye again! Ye are sorely trying my patience!" Mom would be beside herself with weary annoyance. Two min-utes later, we'd hear her again. "I'm coming up now, and I'm coming with the strap!" and then we'd hear the footsteps on the stairs. Thumps loud enough and slow enough to give us time to recover.

At that point there was a mad dash for the beds and the bed-clothes, tucked in tightly at the bottom of the mattresses, were pulled tight up under our chins. As soon as Mom appeared at the door, an almighty bellowing would start.

"Oh please Mom, please, don't hit us. Please, please, stop!" Ellie would be leading the howling chorus, letting on to being murdered in her bed, yelping louder and louder with every feeble slap of the belt on the comforter. "Oh, oh, oh, it hurts! Please, please, stop. We're sorry. We won't do it again." The strap was bouncing off the bedclothes, not going next or near any one of us. But when one howled, we all howled. How our parents put up with this madness night after night and what the roomers thought was going on in the lower quarters of the house is one of the greatest mysteries of all time.

03

IN THIS THREE-STOREY HOUSE, Mom and Dad's bedroom, the kitchen and the living room were all on the ground floor. The first floor could be reached by an interior circular staircase from the ground floor or by the outside stoop. A big double bedroom sat beside the main front door at the top of the stoop and it was occupied by two foreign lady roomers called Maria and Trudy.

Maria was an opera singer, or so we thought, because we could hear her practising her scales — la, la, la, la, la; lo, lo, lo, lo, lo — day and night. Anything that wasn't on Saturday morning's Hit Parade or didn't sound like "Galway Bay" was opera. Plus, Mom and Dad were great fans of Maria Callas, so we considered our Maria to be a class act.

Trudy was Greek and she owned a café on Willis Avenue. At least, we thought she owned it. She was very beautiful and very glamorous with long, silky black hair and she wore tons of make-up. So she must have owned it. Nobody who looked like that could just work in a café. And she had a boyfriend, with a car, who called for her every night and off they would go, all dressed up and smelling of perfume and aftershave. The wonder of it all would take the sight from your eyes.

The top floor of the house was rented to male roomers. One was a short, fat little man that Dad called Scottie, but he was actually from Malta, which made him Italian to us, so why did Dad call him Scottie? The other was a really strange character called Mr Klatz. Where he came from, no one knew. Not even Dad. But he smoked an evil-smelling cigar and he would grunt as he passed us, doing our Saturday morning jobs, like polishing the stair banisters and washing the windows in the lobby. The "lobby". We loved that word. We used it for every room we ever found that didn't have a bed in it.

And then, little by little, the roomers had to leave. The great economic crisis of the 1950s had hit "home" and once again Ireland was disgorging her young by the thousands. Most of them were arriving in the South Bronx and rooms had to be found for them. Every Irish family took its share and these wild and wonderful *"greenhorns"* became part of every household until they secured jobs and could strike out on their own.

We had always known that we weren't true Americans but now we began to understand exactly what we were. We were *"narrowbacks"*. Irish born in America.

ɔʒ

THE FIRST OF THE GREENHORNS to arrive at our breakfast table were the Browns from County Mayo. They were tall and handsome with familiar faces and familiar accents. First came Seán, then his brother Micheál, and finally Máire. But it didn't stop there. The next family to arrive were the Deeleys from County Clare; Mike Deeley and his sister Mary. Mom was mad about all of them but she had a special *grá* for Mike because he was what she called "a little Dandy", and he played a powerful fiddle. Finally, a cousin from County Cork, Kathleen Taaffe, arrived but by then we were packed to the rafters so Kathleen went up to the top of the block to our Aunt Mollie. Our neighbours, the Corcorans and O'Donnells, took the overflow.

The O'Donnells from County Laois were a cut above the rest of us. "Refined" is what Mom called it. Not from Mayo, God Help Us, or Cork or Kerry but the Queen's County of Laois. Oh, and their children's names? Now they were a cut above as well. There was the eldest, Alexander, a perfect gentleman. Then came the tearaway, Edmond, who was the trial of his mother's life, always letting the side down. After that came Robin, if you don't mind, and Charles pronounced Char-les. Then there were the two girls, Nancy, again, and Mary Ann. The O'Donnells kept greenhorns, too, but of a different class. They had the famous Mayo footballer, Pat McAndrews, a giant of a man, and every girl on the street was madly in love with him.

Our neighbours to the bottom of the street were the Kellys from Donegal. They had no greenhorns because they filled the house themselves. There were the Mom and Dad, known as Mammy and Pa to the clan, and then in order of descent, Danny, Patrick, Bernie, Jackie, Clyde, Neil and Kathleen. And they were all of stout mountain stock. If our English was difficult to decipher, theirs was totally unintelligible. It was a mixture of Irish and English with a lilting Donegal accent thrown in.

Mrs Kelly went around all day, delivering orders, with a big, black handbag clutched under her arm. It made no difference if she was cooking the dinner or doing the dishes, the bag never left her arm. We wondered if they had escaped to America with the Crown Jewels and if she was the keeper of the loot. Mr Kelly was never seen without a hammer in his hand, forever adding bits of extensions to the rear of the house. Every evening when the banging started, Dad would let out an exasperated wail: "Oh, Sacred Heart of God, Old Man Kelly has found a few more nails."

Mrs O'Donnell was not happy at all with the presence of the Kellys on her doorstep. They were always up to some sort of devilment and they had us, the O'Connells, in collusion with them.

The railway line ran along the edge of our neighbourhood but we were not supposed to go off our street. After all, it was a world unto itself, so where was the need? We must have had a few dozen nationalities of every size, age, colour and religion, forever jostling for position and living life to the hilt. But the railway line held a hidden trove of treasure, discovered only by the crafty Kellys — discarded orange crates.

The fruit and vegetable market also ran along the railway line. Every family had its favourite vendor and ours was called Sal. He carried the potatoes, turnips and parsnips, which other sellers, who catered for different cultural needs, neglected. But what they all had in common was oranges. And the disused crates held out enormous potential.

Mrs O'Donnell became outraged one evening when she spotted Jackie and Danny Kelly pushing a child's red wagon up the street and it piled high with broken crates. They were heading for the Kelly's aireyway, where they unloaded the cache and began tinkering around with the broken bits of soft wood. Out came Old Man Kelly's hammer and nails. The indecency of it all! It was quite bad enough when they were at that carry-on out of sight, in the privacy of their own backyard. But to bring it into public view was going too far. She would have to have a word with Mrs O'Connell.

Before she had a chance to lower the boom, Danny and Jackie had constructed a very passable footstool from one of the orange crates and presented it to our Mom. She was tickled pink and told the young men that they were so good, they should go into business for themselves. So the daily trek to the railway yard became routine. Footstools were made in the aireyway and sold in the market. The boys soon graduated to bedside lockers and when those took off, they abandoned the aireyway and rented a storeroom.

Danny and Jackie had left school in Ireland at primary level but what they lacked in education they more than made up for in talent and drive. When the range of furniture items began to outstrip orange crate dimensions, they began to buy in lumber, and then a delivery truck was needed. Danny became the business manager, Bernie the driver, and Jackie the craftsman.

Business was booming. New immigrants were arriving in the South Bronx from the Caribbean, especially from Puerto Rico, and the Kellys took a lease on an abandoned warehouse uptown, around East 149th Street. Expansion meant a change of direction.

The Kelly boys cut back on the production of furniture and began to import it. Kelly's Furniture Store became one of the first Bronx businesses to offer "buying on time". A small deposit and monthly payments with interest secured a bed, a sofa or any one of the newest arrivals on the furniture scene — a washing machine or maybe even a television set.

But success had brought its own problems: who would manage the accounts and the legal business when clients defaulted on their payments? Why, Clyde and Neil, of course. As the younger members of the clan grew up, Clyde was sent to Manhattan College and Neil graduated from Fordham University. The thorny issues of accountancy and law had now been securely factored in.

Robbie O'Donnell was eventually ordained a priest and Danny Kelly, along with his cohort Emmett O'Connell, were later inducted into the Order of St Gregory, the highest honour that can be bestowed on lay Catholics by the papacy. A priest and two papal knights from three neighbouring houses in the South Bronx! I think even Mrs O'Donnell would have approved.

Kelly's Furniture Store became an institution in the Bronx, Queens and Brooklyn, and the entire Donegal-born Kelly family eventually abandoned East 139th Street for the genteel and leafy quarters of Westchester County.

Kathleen Kelly never had to work. Kathleen Kelly became a lady.

 times

ST JEROME'S WAS OUR PARISH CHURCH and it was located on Alexander Avenue, the Fifth Avenue of the Bronx. Brook Avenue had the subway station, the Chinese laundry, Whelan's Drug Store, Harry's Grocery, the Curtain Store, Mrs English's Candy Store, the German Deli and the Cigar Store. Willis Avenue had the Casino Movie Theatre, Cushman's Bakery, Nick & Tessie's Candy Store, Trudy's Diner, Mr Baumblatt's, Photographer, and the Star of Munster Ballroom. Alexander Avenue had St Jerome's Church, St Jerome's Boys' School, St Jerome's Girls' School, the 40th Precinct Police Station, the public library, platoons of private stately homes, whispering trees and no greenhorns.

St Jerome's Church, known as the Cathedral of the South Bronx, was a marvel of Gothic architecture with its imperial spires rising into the skies to prick the very heavens. St Jerome, an early Christian doctor of the church, sat high on the church edifice, open book in his hands, gazing down in all his wisdom at the renegade bands of children running to school along Alexander Avenue. Many a child's knee was grazed as he raced by, hastily genuflecting at the statue, fearful that he would be struck down if he dared to pass without showing due reverence.

The Catholic Church had a massive influence on all of our lives. When we moved up the block to Number 445, we transferred from PS 9 to St Jerome's Parochial School. The Ursuline Sisters ran the Girls' School and the Irish Christian Brothers ran the Boys' School. There was no such thing as co-education for Bronx Irish Catholics. In fact, we were ruled with an iron hand and there was no velvet glove in sight.

Monsignor Patrick J. O'Donnell was our parish priest and he carried an aura that put the fear of God into us all. He was an elderly man with a booming voice. He always appeared on the altar in the most exquisitely handcrafted church vestments with layers of white lace peeking out from under the gold embroidered surplices. And there was an added mystique to this ensemble: the fuchsia-coloured skull cap of the Monsignor. "What magnificent thing has he done for the Lord to warrant that?" we often wondered.

Every Easter Monday, a special Communion Mass was held at St Jerome's Church to mark the Dublin Easter Rising of 1916. Monsignor O'Donnell ritually addressed the faithful, the church packed as it was with exiled members of the IRA. He was an outspoken Irish Republican and given to delivering incendiary sermons from the pulpit on such auspicious occasions. Consequently, he had been cautioned by the higher-ranking Cardinal to "tone it down" a little.

Easter Monday came and Monsignor was up in the pulpit in full flight, relating the story of the Last Supper. "And as Christ looked around at his disciples," whispered Monsignor, "He told them that there was one in their midst who was soon to betray Him." Monsignor stopped and gazed deep into the congregation before continuing. "Is it I, Lord?" asked a querulous John. "No," replied Christ, "It is not you." "Is it I, then?" asked Simon, looking straight into the eyes of the Lord. Once again Christ replied, "No, it is not you." And then Judas spoke up: "Oy, Guv, I say, is it I?"

It's a tough old station, this loyalty to God, Cardinal and cause! Monsignor seemed to juggle them all particularly well. Maybe that's why he had the fuchsia hat.

Church was a place to be taken deadly seriously. When you genuflected, there was no scraping of the knee across the kneeler, no lame half-bending and flight. You went straight down to the floor, whether you were eight or eighty. Mass was in Latin and we learnt the entire Mass off by heart, every last Deo Gratias and Dominus Vobiscum, although that particular phrase often got spat out as "Dominic, would ya frisk 'em?"

We were true evangelists before we ever knew the meaning of the word. We could discuss the mysteries of our faith and the meaning of transubstantiation when we were no more than children. Our heroes were discovered in the lives of the saints and the early martyrs. Maria Goretti, a young fifteen-year-old Italian martyr who died protecting her virginity, was canonised in the 1950s. What followed was a rash of South Bronx newborns being christened Goretti. We had Goretti O'Brien and Goretti Burns on our block. First Holy Communion and Confirmation were true rites of passage. The Baltimore Catechism had to be learnt off by heart. Our Daily Prayers were as familiar to our tongues as our own names and the mysteries of the rosary were recited in school with daily fervour.

These were the days when Father Patrick Peyton's Family Rosary Crusade was sweeping the nation. Every Friday afternoon, one student in each class was chosen to take home the classroom statue of the Virgin Mary for the weekend. The student entrusted with the statue was instructed to make sure that the family recited the rosary every night and he or she was cautioned to return the statue promptly to the classroom on Monday morning.

This frequently caused all kinds of consternation in our house. With five children attending Catholic schools, the moving Marys were making their visits to our house with alarming regularity.

Family meant everybody in the house — mother, father and children included. But this particular BIC family was not very big into outward displays of religious fervour. Showy rituals should be confined to the church. So the idea of getting down on our knees every night at home to recite the rosary was going to be problematic, to say the least.

First, there was the delicate issue of Dad. Dad attended Mass every Sunday and every holy day of obligation. He fulfilled his Easter obligations and he didn't eat meat on Fridays. He didn't go to church processions, he didn't say prayers before meals and he didn't recite Father Peyton's family rosary. As far as the clergy were concerned, his favourite expression became, "You have to keep them on a short lead."

Oh my God! What were we to do? Say the rosary ourselves and pretend that Dad had been part of it — or tell the truth and shame the devil?

We said the rosary ourselves, with Mom making a gallant effort to keep order among the five of us. We would start off in pretty good form, trying our level best to be holy and devout. But every time we stole a peek at one another, mooching around on our knees on the cold kitchen floor, or, whenever we caught sight of the actor Ellie with her long, mournful face pondering over her string of brown beads, our muffled sniggering would begin. As the rosary continued, with Mom leading the recitation of Hail Marys and Our Fathers and the rest of us trying valiantly to respond, a chorus of strangled guffaws would begin to escape. We would rapidly lose all control and end up howling out loud, with tears of laughter streaming down our faces. Mom would be bucking with barely contained rage. "Blasphemers is what ye are. The very cheek of ye! Blasphemers, one and all. May God forgive ye, and his blessed Mother in heaven. Look at the state of ye, falling around the floor in kinks in the middle of the Five Sorrowful Mysteries!"

This was just not for us. This kind of stuff was for Baptists and Evangelists. They simply loved holding hands around the dinner table and bowing their heads at the drop of a hat. We didn't even like doing that in church.

So we told the truth and shamed the devil. Mary kept coming to our house but Mom gave up on trying to direct the family rosary. She told us to say it to ourselves. "Meditate in silence, please!"

However, any kind of private reticence for family prayer did nothing to dampen our enthusiasm for the aura of church rituals. We all had favourite parts of the Mass and mine came after the Mass when Monsignor O'Donnell offered Benediction. The silent church would become even more silent as Monsignor walked slowly to the side of the altar, removed a voluminous cape from an intricately carved and highly polished clothes horse, draped it carefully around his shoulders and returned solemnly to the centre of the altar to raise the magnificent golden monstrance to the congregation. A battalion of privileged altar boys standing at the side altar busily filled silver incense burners, which hung from long metal chains. Then they floated to the centre altar and, facing the monstrance, they began to swing the burners; back and forth, back and forth. The jangling of the chains and the opening and closing of the burners moved with perfect rhythm, one, two, three, one, two, three, one, two three, as the sweet and intoxicating smell of frankincense filled the church. Being a Catholic was a truly amazing thing!

Ꮸ

BACK ON 139TH STREET, the O'Connells were turning their attention to music. Spurred on by the fiddle playing of Mike Deeley and accordion playing of Micheál Brown, I had taken up the violin, Gretta was on the button accordion and Eleanor was singing away like a lark.

The entire extended family, including all the aunts, uncles and cousins from all sides of the family, celebrated every single Christening, First Communion, Confirmation and Graduation. That meant more or less an event every weekend, considering the numbers involved. Sometimes the party was held in Brooklyn, at Uncle Tim's, if it were an O'Connell event, or it could be in Woodside or the Bronx in the case of a Taaffe event. For the South Bronx Five, travelling to the gathering was the best part of all because we got to go for a ride on the subway.

First, we would all line up in front of the ticket window to get the right change. There would be Mom and Aunt Mollie Ferreira, who lived up the street from us with our cousin, Little Johnny. Aunt Mollie's husband, Big Johnny, was a merchant seaman and he was usually away in some distant place like Vladivostok or Venezuela. We learned a lot of geography from Big Johnny, who brought us back exotic items like "hot tamales" whenever he returned. We added that to our list of questionable cultural delicacies, along with the DiMaggio figs and dates. Dad rarely made it to these excursions. He was always either recovering from work or working.

We approached these outings with a mixture of excitement and dread; the excitement came from standing beside the motorman's cab, our hearts thumping as the train sped through long, dark tunnels, the cold, dank wind stinging our eyes and whipping our long hair around our faces. Then came the deafening screech of brakes as the train thundered into a station. Dread came when the jostling and jolting became too much for our stomachs. We would invariably become travel sick and poor Mom would have to hold our heads as, one by one, we got deathly sick onto the tracks.

All would be forgotten when we finally arrived at our destination. Inside our aunt's our uncle's house, the adults would sit together gossiping and telling tales from "home" while the older cousins like the Walshes, O'Keeffes and Bunces worked away in the kitchen, preparing the food. We younger ones entertained ourselves, huddled around song books that came out every month and trying out the latest hits. Edith Piaf was all the rage with her hit, "La Vie en Rose", in the charts. That and "With A Song in My Heart" were Ellie's high-flyers.

When we tired of that, out would come the Classic Comics. Classical stories from the old masters, like *Oliver Twist*, *Gulliver's Travels* and *Treasure Island*, were printed in comic-book style and were bought, collected and traded among anyone able to read. We read and re-read the stories until we were word perfect and then we retold the tales ourselves, waiting to catch one another out whenever someone went wrong or missed a part. Ellie was the princess of storytime, acting out one part after another and never letting anyone else get a look in.

After the food had been eaten and the tea drunk, the real entertainment would begin. All the children had their party pieces prepared. Kevin had a stunning voice and he would start the ball rolling with the number one song from Your Hit Parade, "Ghost Riders in the Sky". Emmett was next up with a moving oration of

Robert Emmet's speech from the dock, or sometimes, when he was in form, he would thrill us with "Kelly the Boy from Killane". Then Ellie would take the floor with "The Isle of Innisfree". After that bit of tearful balladry had been suitably received, Johnny Ferreira would launch into a rousing rendition of "The Minstrel Boy", having learnt it for the school choir's performance at the Fordham College *Feis*.

A break would then commence, with the parents doing their part by engaging in a series of *"cumauyees"*, which in later years I discovered to actually be "come all ye". These were old-time music hall songs that began with "Come all ye fair young maidens" and so on, songs that everyone could sing along with. One, as I recall, began with "Mush, mush, mush too-ra-lie-ad-ee", and ended up with some unfortunate miscreant being thrown into the back of a calaboose.

Ω

I WAS LEARNING THE VIOLIN at the time from a silenced priest called Father Costello who lived in a house all by himself on East 135th Street. Father Costello scared the living daylights out of me. He was tall and thin and very stern, and maybe Spanish, because he spoke with an unfamiliar accent. He was always dressed in his black surplice, with it trailing along the floor like a black stream and following him wherever he went like a big, black shadow.

I would arrive at his house with my violin twice a week, be admitted by his housekeeper, and then proceed into the front room where a music stand stood beside a high-backed chair and a desk. The room was always dark, even on the sunniest days. Father would come in, silently nod to me, take my music copy from me and begin composing notes, his fingers flowing across the page like music itself, the little black circles with their curlicue flags appearing like magic in just the right places. Then he would take me through my scales, rapping my fingers with the tip of a pencil whenever I hit the wrong note.

I never knew what it meant to be silenced, only that it was very sad and all the mothers felt very sorry for him. I just figured that it had something to do with those pesky politics again! So loads of us were sent along for lessons because he didn't have a parish to support him. Consequently, my party piece, for a very long time, became a series of stuttering scales. The relatives must have been blessed with great forbearance to sit through that painful performance, week after week. And Gretta got to complete the session with a recitation of the 48 states — in alphabetical order — and sometimes she even delivered them backwards.

ය

GRETTA WAS THE YOUNGEST CHILD in the family and an instigating little street scrapper at that. Every day she would be primped and preened by Mom, all dressed up in buttons and bows, and set loose upon the world with the salutary caution to *behave yourself!* But her pouting little cherubic face masked a veritable demon hiding inside. No devilment was beyond her. No sooner would she have hit the street than we would hear old Mrs Esposito roaring from her window in the apartments across the way, "Go home you little wretch. There you go again. A villain, that's what you are. You're a menace to society. Go home, I tell you."

And Gretta would be out there in the middle of the street, spoiling for trouble, mitts up in front of that pudgy little face and it turning redder and redder by the second. "Come on, you scairdy cat. You wan-na *fight?*" She was plain loco, challenging Annie King to a fistfight. Annie was twice her size and Annie could *fight.* In no time flat, the bows would be reefed from Gretta's bouncing pigtails and her hair sent flying in all directions. Then the howling would begin and Ellie would come tearing down the street like the hammers of hell. Nobody, but nobody, messed with Ellie, not even Annie King. Ellie would bring Gretta limping home, her hair in disarray and tears streaming down her dirty little face. She never learnt. Next day, she would be out there again at the same old carry-on, only to come home once more with her head in her hands.

Something had to be done to keep Gretta out of trouble, so she was put on the button accordion. The accordion was bigger than herself but she attacked it as though it were Annie King, huffing and puffing as she struggled to pull the bellows in and out. This was great *craic*, especially when she got to lug it around in its big black case, looking oh-so-important and sticking out her tongue at poor Annie as she sat sullenly on her stoop.

Then, when she tired of the accordion, she decided she would simply be sensational on the snare drums, you know, as lead drummer for the Bob Barrett Pipe and Drum Band. This was even greater *craic*, as she got to hammer the life out of a goatskin and be considered talented for doing it. But at least the street fighting stopped and Mom's head got a bit of peace.

CB

AUNT ANNETTE O'CONNELL, Dad's sister who had been sent out to Texas in her youth to become a nun, had leapt the wall and become a registered nurse instead. After having worked for some time as a public health nurse in the state of Georgia, she had joined the US Army. Fancy that! From child lookout for marauding Black and Tans in the hills of Sligo to Captain with the American armed forces in occupied Germany. That cultural leap must occasionally have put her head spinning!

Aunt Annette's rare visits to the Bronx sparked off as much excitement as the St Patrick's Day Parade. Here was a true touch of class, true glamour the likes of which had never before been seen on East 139th Street.

Aunt Annette was a grown-up version of our sister Eleanor; the same mass of red-blonde hair, the sky-blue eyes and the flawless Dresden complexion. But she carried with her a worldly air that mystified us. She wore the bottle-green uniform of an army Captain, with knee-length skirt and fitted jacket, crème starched shirt and matching green tie. It was the brown leather bag, however, hanging ever so casually from her trim shoulders that captivated us. That, the army hat cocked to the side of her head and the seductive Southern drawl. I don't ever remember actually talking to Aunt Annette — just staring and listening in rapt *stupefication*.

og

ELEANOR WAS THE ONE AMONGST US with the real, blinding talent and it became evident at a very young age. She would often sit in front of the mirror in Mom's bedroom, brushing her billowing blond tresses and reciting some new bit of gibberish that she had just heard on the radio. As Dad passed by, he would throw her a quizzical look, with the murmured aside, "Vanity, vanity, didst I ever offend thee!" Ellie would just carry on, slipping effortlessly from Gene Kelly's "Singin' in the Rain" to one of Al Martino's latest hits.

Ellie was the apple of Dad's eye. Every Saturday night, he would spend hours wrapping her hair in ringlet rags in preparation for Sunday Mass while he quizzed the rest of us on our school spellings. Already, we were heading off in different directions.

Ellie never doubted that she would some day be famous. We would lie awake for hours, after the dust had settled on our madcap escapades, to begin our next night-time exercise — dreaming up new and fantastic-sounding names for her impending stardom. Eleanor O'Connell just would not do — it was so — well, Irish! And we needed something exciting and wonderful and foreign for the lights of Broadway. Lorna Doone was lovely, but Kevin reminded us that it was already taken. So, Desiree Doon became the frontrunner for a long time, Desiree being the beautiful and tragic heroine of the Napoleon Bonaparte sagas. Then, along came Eiana Rockneen. We just made that one up, pure fantasy. We must have inherited a lot of Mom's genes, because it just sounded really nice. But Ellie was a hard one to please. She needed something stronger, not just musical and airy-fairy. So we finally hit on Gale Storm. Now if there weren't enough power and force in that name, well I'd just eat my hat!

CƷ

GRETTA AND I HAD BEGUN TAKING Irish step-dancing classes at the Star of Munster Ballroom on East 138th Street when we were about ten or eleven years old. Our teacher was Bob Barrett from County Cork. Professor Barrett, as we correctly called him, was a musician as well as a dancing teacher. Come to think of it, he was a bit of a genius. He taught step-dancing, violin, accordion, bagpipes, tin whistle and drums and he organised a group of us into the Bob Barrett School of Irish Dancing.

We were an ensemble way ahead of our time. *Riverdance* wasn't even a mild hallucination when we were step-dancing our way across the Bronx and into Long Island and beyond. We even went to Boston on the midnight train special. The whole month of March was taken up with glorious St Patrick's Day events. And when we entertained at parish socials on Saturday nights, we received special dispensations from the parish priests so we could drink water after midnight and still be able to receive Holy Communion on Sunday morning! That was known as "breaking the fast" and it was a rare and wonderful privilege.

Our ultimate moment of glory came when we appeared on the "Ted Mack Amateur Hour" on television and won first place on three consecutive Sunday nights. As our prize, each one of the troupe received a wristwatch for each of the winning performances. So where Dad had been the only one with a wristwatch in our family before that little adventure, now every O'Connell was sporting a new Bulova timepiece.

The St Patrick's Day Parade was a red-letter day on every calendar in every Irish household in New York City. That was the day when we owned the city, the day we could take over the subway system and strut our stuff.

The level of excitement reached fever pitch on the eve of the
great day, as we laid out our band uniforms on the beds. Our
green velveteen jackets were bedecked with rows and rows of
gold (plated), silver (plated), and bronze (plated) medals, clear
evidence of mastery in Irish song, music and dance and trium-
phantly secured against massive competition at *feiseanna* all over
the northeast. We had long since left the fiddles and accordions
behind and were now seriously into bagpipes and drums. There
was no limit to where our parents would take us, provided music
was on the agenda.

Mom was the original *feis* mother, wrapping our hair in rags to
make the regulation ringlets, washing and bleaching our white
socks and packing our dancing and band uniforms for weekend
trips to Boston, the Catskill Mountains or New Jersey. We still had
no television, no telephone and no car but we had every musical
instrument known to man. We had a violin, two button accordions, a set of bagpipes, tin whistles, a snare drum, a guitar and we
were working on getting a piano.

The biggest day of the year started off bright and early and it
was usually snowing a blizzard or blowing up a storm. We'd run
up to the top of the block to see the County Corkmen's Pipe Band
tuning up before they set off for East 42nd Street. Then it was back
home and into our uniforms. Dad was always magnificent on this
special day, decked out in his long black wool overcoat and his
steel-grey felt hat, with a sprig of real shamrock tucked into the
band around the brim. He had a large touch of class himself and
this was his finest hour.

Parading proudly down to the Brook Avenue station, we
would join hordes of others who were heading downtown, with
bagpipes wailing and drums pounding and the stirring airs of
"Garryowen" and "O'Donnell Abu" blaring out to thunderous
applause. As the train careered along its journey, crowds of Spanish and Black Americans joined the crush, their green hair and
green shamrocked faces shocking the senses.

We had to be in front of St Patrick's Cathedral before noon because Uncle Tim was at the head of the parade. He would be coming up Fifth Avenue with the New York City Mounted Police and taking the salute from Cardinal Spellman as the Cardinal stood on the cathedral steps surrounded by the mayor, the police chief and dozens of dignitaries. We nearly cried with excitement as Uncle Tim came into view, looking so proud and elegant on his magnificent horse. Then it was a race up to 48th Street to join our own contingent. We had evolved from dancing troupe into the Bob Barrett Pipe Band and we were invariably attached to some organisation in need of a marching band for the day. The ritual ended with us returning home to Mom, blue with the cold, totally exhausted and starving with hunger, and with "The Rakes of Mallow" embedded forever in our psyche.

೧

WHEN EMMETT, ELLIE, GRETTA AND I were enrolled at St Jerome's Parochial School on Alexander Avenue, Kevin, for some mysterious reason, was sent up the hill to St Luke's. This meant that he had to walk in a different direction from the rest of us and, what's more, he began moving with some very suspect and slightly seditious company. His walk took him past Mrs English's Ice Cream Parlour on Brook Avenue, it being a notorious hangout for all the cool dudes of the neighbourhood. So it wasn't long before Kevin began sporting nine-inch pegged pants that strangled his ankles, and pushing his luck with shocking pink dress shirts and long stringy chartreuse neckties.

New York City was in a league of its own. Everything happened earlier and faster in New York. Long before the "rock and roll" era descended on the rest of the world, "zoot-suiters" were struttin' their stuff around the Bronx.

Kevin was even spotted, once or twice, sipping chocolate egg creams in the ice cream parlour with money cadged from his after-school deli job. Big trouble was surely lurking round the corner.

That trouble usually erupted every evening around 5.00 pm, when Kevin failed to appear for dinner. As dusk began to fall, I retreated to my bedroom and hid myself behind a stack of books in a vain attempt to ward off the inevitable. "Gerry," I would hear my Mom calling from downstairs, "go down and get your brother before your father gets home." My helpless wails forever fell on deaf ears. "Please Mom, don't make me. You know I hate going down there." But it was all to no avail. I had to go.

I could feel my face glowing like red hot coals as I stood in the doorway of Mrs English's Ice-Cream Parlour scanning the darkness for my brother. A collection of suave, slicked-back male heads milled around the neon flashing lights of a pulsating jukebox that sat in the corner. Pony-tails bobbed as bright young girls in matching twin sets and ballooning crinoline skirts spun around to the latest dance crazes, such as the lindy-hop, with their slim hands and long legs flailing the air. I was barely noticed, standing there in my black-and-white saddle shoes and buttoned-up school gabardine.

Having caught my brother's eye, I would flee into the gathering dusk with Kevin following close on my heels. We had to get home and slip into our chairs before Dad arrived to cast a knowing scowl over the potential jailbird in our midst, with the terse enquiry, "So what did *you* do today to justify your existence?"

But Kevin successfully graduated from Cardinal Hayes High School without ever falling foul of the law. And then he did the most outrageous of things. He traded in his pegged pants for rubber galoshes and entered Farmingdale Agricultural Institute on Long Island to learn how to be a farmer. Of all the crazy ideas, this one took the biscuit. A kid from the South Bronx wanting to be a farmer!

Kevin spent two years out there, finding out all about the secrets of battery-hatched chickens and the intricacies of animal husbandry, and then, when he had just received his agricultural degree, he was drafted into the United States Army. He would become the most conservative, the most truly American of us all.

Following six weeks of basic training at Fort Dix Camp in New Jersey, Kevin was sent abroad to a place called Wiesbaden in West Germany and from there he began making his first visits "home" to Sligo. In his company went his buddy, Ralph Brancaccio, and the two young American GIs, resplendent in their sharp, crisp army uniforms made quite a splash in the depressed Ireland of the mid-1950s.

03

THEN ONE DAY, CLEAR OUT OF THE BLUE, we were told that we too were going "home". Was that what they had been cooking up in the kitchen, in hushed tones, all those nights while we stood outside looking in? It didn't make any sense.

How could we being going to Ireland? We hadn't inherited a fortune. We hadn't won the Irish Sweepstakes. We didn't own a car or even a television set. Television was fast becoming a national craze but we didn't have one. We would all have to troop up to Aunt Mollie's house on Tuesday evenings to sit on her sofa, jammed in tightly beside one another, and watch the "Milton Berle Show". This manic comedian with the mad voices and crazy faces was the toast of the town. Everyone was talking about Milton Berle, everyone was getting cars and television sets, everyone except us.

Nonetheless, we were heading off on the United States Line's *SS America* for a six-day voyage to Ireland. Emmett, Gretta and I. And what's more, we were going alone.

03

Chapter 4

HOMEWARD BOUND

IT REALLY WAS ALL LIKE A DREAM. The farthest away that we had ever been was to the *feis* in Boston. Now we were heading across the Atlantic in a huge ocean liner, just like Park Avenue bluebloods! The great day arrived. It was early June, 1955. Mom and Dad took us to the West Side Shipping Terminal by taxi, with our bags and two big wooden crates. Everything was checked in and we were shown to our cabins, dizzy with excitement. Just before departure, Dad handed Emmett instructions about what we were to do when we reached the other side.

We were to take the train from Cobh to Killarney where we were to disembark and go directly to a certain bed-and-breakfast. The owners were friends and they would be expecting us. But we were only staying there one night, because the next day we were to travel on by train to Limerick and book into Cruise's Hotel. And surprise, surprise! Dad would be flying into Shannon and he would meet us there. Dad hadn't been back to Ireland since he had left, all those years before. People didn't just up and visit Ireland in the 1950s. Why were we? Things were just getting crazier and crazier but we took it all in our stride. We were used to all kinds of eventualities. There had never been anything straightforward in our lives. Why should it be any different now?

Gretta and I were sharing a cabin with two sisters, the Donovans, from Evanston, Illinois, and Emmett was next door, sharing with their brothers. The whole Donovan family was travelling to

Europe for this European experience and the first stop was to be Ireland. Man, were they nutters! The Mom would bounce into our cabin first thing in the morning with a mad cry, "Wakey, wake-y! Rise and shine! Hit the deck! Greet the new day! A new day is dawning! Hallelujah!" Mamma mia! What kind of talk was that? But they were real Americans so we guessed it was allowed. And what's more, they really did live on Elm Street.

We threw ourselves into life aboard ship with gusto, making friends with the ship's purser and stewards and thereby gaining admission to facilities way beyond our station — the first class deck with its deckside shuffleboard and heated swimming pool.

It was also on this voyage that we were finally disabused of any notion we might still be harbouring that we were Irish-Americans. We were firmly and emphatically told by the ship's officers, when nationality was requested, that we were either Irish or American, but there was no such thing as a hyphenated American. And since we carried American passports, like it or not, we were Americans.

This was a lethal blow to our sense of self, to our identity, to our whole understanding of who we were. It was like being told we were orphans, that we had been adopted, that we weren't really who we thought we were, that we were, in fact, total frauds. We were, after all, as American as Sally, Dick and Jane. It was just too much to take in.

The *SS America* pulled into Cobh Harbour late at night, so we dropped anchor out in the bay and prepared to wait overnight for customs and immigration officers to come on board. Passengers leaving the ship at Cobh had to be cleared by both departments before disembarking. The ship would then proceed on to Southampton for its final port of call.

We spent a fitful night, twisting and turning and waiting for dawn. With the breaking of first light, we were out of our beds and up on deck. The sun's faint rays singed a lingering mist and slowly, steadily the outline of shore came into view. What we saw

was a serenely sloping landscape with slumbering houses se-
creted together, their soft lights glowing like gentle guardians of
all they surveyed.

We were soon joined on deck by the gasping Donovans, their
"Oh, my Gods" and "Golly, gees" shattering the stillness of the
dawn. A flotilla of small vessels appeared on the water, heading
towards our ship, and led by the customs and immigration officers in their smart gold-braided navy uniforms. Since the landing
pier was too shallow to accommodate ocean liners like the *America*, our baggage would be cleared on board and then taken ashore
on trawlers. Passengers would follow shortly after that on several
small ferries.

All personal belongings were loaded into the ballroom and
passenger lounges for inspection. Customs men passed along the
heaps of bags, boxes and trunks, questioning owners about the
contents, casting a cursory peek into the occasional case and
marking everything with a bit of chalk. We stood beside our baggage, chatted with the friendly officers about our first trip
"home", and then with these technicalities out of the way, we
joined the long queues awaiting disembarkation. Our Irish adventure was about to begin.

The one and only drawback to this budding adventure was the
cursed load of baggage we were carting along with us. It was only
as we were trying to load it onto the Killarney-bound train that
we realised how much and how heavy it all was. "Good God Almighty, how are we going to manage to drag all of this stuff from
Killarney to Limerick and from there on to Sligo?" we moaned.
But Dad hadn't been home in over twenty years, so we figured
that he must have bought presents for the whole of the county.

On the train to Killarney, a very funny thing happened. From
out of nowhere, a complete stranger approached us and said directly to me, "Ahrah, geh-rl, you must be one of Jackie Taaffe's
daughters. Sure, I'd know those Taaffe eyes anywhere." I had to
tell him that I was, in fact, Jackie Taaffe's niece but that I had

never met him and that this was my first visit to Ireland. He was as astounded as I. Here I was, 3,000 miles away from where I was born, but immediately recognisable as part of a family I had never met. Only four days earlier, I had been told that I couldn't possibly be Irish. But accidents of birth do not the genes diminish. Of that, I was now sure.

The transfer from train to boarding house began to demonstrate just how difficult this trip was going to be. "The Lord preserve us," said the taxi man as he struggled to haul the heavy cases into the boot of his car. "What have ye packed in here, lads? Lead?" We fell around the place laughing. How preposterous. The very idea of three American teenagers heading for the fabled Lakes of Killarney with trunks full of lead!

This whole sorry episode was repeated at the boarding house, with curses and swears turning the air blue as we pushed and heaved the cases up the stairs. "This is nuts," mumbled Emmett, sweating and panting with his delicate heart. "Totally crazy! What the blazes has Dad been thinkin' loading us down like this? And we're only supposed to be here one night. We're outta here in the mornin'. But we'll be notorious by then. What taxi man in his right mind will want to carry us with our leaden cases?"

But we needn't have worried. Not at all. A few hours after our arrival, two lovely young men arrived at the boarding house, said they had been expecting us and relieved us of all our very heavy luggage. We were free to carry on, light-footed and light of bags. Magic! Regardless of what the ship's captain might think, we knew we were Irish-Americans and being Irish-American was a truly amazing thing.

So carry on we did. On to Limerick and Shannon Airport where we were on hand to greet our Dad on his first visit home. How strange that must have been for him, to be met in the land of his birth by his own children. And they having just completed a mysterious mission, totally unbeknownst to themselves. He, "The Keeper of the Flame", had managed to pull off a miracle of planning. But my, oh my! How Ireland and the world have now changed!

It was only in later years that I began to wonder why Eleanor had not been included on that trip, and it was much later that I began to fit the pieces of the jigsaw together. Eleanor was temperamental. Eleanor was highly charged. Eleanor was inquisitive. Eleanor might have let the cat out of the bag.

ℭ

THE NEXT COUPLE OF MONTHS were a twister of frenetic activity, though our Dad only stayed for a couple of weeks. We travelled on together to Aunt Della's — Della Hennigan being a *grande dame* of Sligo Town and licensed vintner at Hennigans of Wine Street.

Aunt Della was a handsome woman, not pretty in a fluffy, comely sense but tall and striking with the strong O'Connell bones. She had been widowed for several years and was being actively pursued by every eligible bachelor of a certain age in the county of Sligo. Chief amongst her suitors was a retired sea captain, snappy in his trim blues and waxed moustache. And Della kept them all guessing, content to hold court from behind the bar, charming everyone and favouring no one. Every Saturday evening she dispatched us off to the Atlantic Hotel in Bundoran, aboard the CIE Dance Bus, to join whatever youth were left in the West and return with detailed reports of anyone we might have met whom "we liked better than ourselves".

Two of our favourite cousins in County Sligo were Hal Hennigan, son of the daunting Della, and Fidelma Flynn, daughter of Aunt Gretta and Garda Sergeant Pat Flynn. We tucked that little piece of information carefully away in our family memory banks to retrieve, in later years, whenever the debates raging around Irish republicanism would become over-heated in our South Bronx kitchen. Pat Flynn was a kindly, gentle man and we would find it hard to reconcile our Dad's mixed emotions regarding the Garda Síochána with this sterling representative of the Irish police force. But for Dad, it was always the "principle" that mattered; personalities were never part of the equation.

Hal Hennigan was a few years younger than ourselves but he was already a student at Summerhill College. "How can that be?" we wondered amongst ourselves. A college student at the age of thirteen? But with an exquisitely well-tuned and cultivated voice accompanied by a bewildering ability to finish every conversation, no matter how mundane, with just the right quotation from William Butler Yeats or James Joyce, we concluded that he was some sort of child genius.

That is, until our still younger cousin, Fidelma, enlightened us about the peculiarities of Hiberno-English. The Irish equivalent to American high school was college and an American college would be an Irish university. And that was just the beginning. An Irish biscuit was an American cookie, a mineral in Sligo was a soda in the Bronx, we went to the pictures in Sligo and to the movies in New York, jumpers were really sweaters and pinafores were jumpers and the runners on our feet would go back to being sneakers in America. Then Dad finished the language lesson. While American Republicans were defenders of the American "union" and very wealthy capitalists, Irish republicans were separatists and defenders of the working class. What then would Irish "unionists" be?

Our grasp of the English language was getting more tenuous by the minute!

೫

THE SUPERNATURAL FORCES of war and peace, love, envy and fate transcend human form and soar above the tranquil hills of Knocknarea, in the County of Sligo. In the great epics of ancient Ireland, a vibrant spirit world lives side by side with natural life, often nurturing it but sometimes sending evil spirits to upset the best-laid plans of human kind. That Ireland of long ago is a highly charged society throbbing with all the energies of physical challenges, clan jealousies, greed, glorious wars, tragic defeats and heroic deaths. On one midsummer's morning, Hal and Fidelma, Dad, Emmett, Gretta and I set out on our bicycles for the hills overlooking Sligo Bay. And as we lay our bikes against a tree and began the long but gentle climb to the summit of Knocknarea, Dad told us the story of her great Celtic warrior queen, Queen Maeve.

Maeve was the beautiful and much-adored daughter of the High King of Ireland. On reaching maturity, at the age of twenty-one, she demanded a whole province of Ireland to rule over. "Very well," said her father, the High King, "You shall have the Province of Connacht."

And so the new Queen Maeve of Connacht built a magnificent palace of gleaming white stone at Cruachán on the far western shores of Ireland. She filled it with treasures of gold and silver and raised an army of servants to wait upon her and an army of warriors to fight for her. But her greatest treasures of all grazed in the fields around her palace, her magnificent herds of prize cattle.

Maeve was a fiery and tempestuous ruler, often leading her army into fierce battles against any chieftain who might dare to displease her. After rejecting scores of hopeful suitors who came to pay homage and ask for her hand, she fell in love with and married the haughty Ailill, son of the mighty King of Leinster.

Ailill brought all of his treasures and herds of horses, sheep and cattle to Cruachan and began to pride himself on being the richest person in Ireland. When Maeve heard this, she immediately threw down a challenge. "Display all that you possess, Ailill, and I vow I shall prove that I am wealthier than you."

Queen Maeve and Ailill, Son of the King of Leinster, matched each other, goblet to goblet, gold to gold, silver to silver, horse to horse, sheep to sheep and cow to cow and found that they were exactly equal. That is, until Ailill produced a magnificent bull named Finnbeannach. Maeve shook with rage. She had no animal to match him.

Calling her Chief Messenger, Mac Roth, to her chamber, she demanded to know where she could find a bull to match Finnbeannach. "In Ulster," replied Mac Roth, "there is a much finer animal known as the Brown Bull of Cooley. But King Conor will never let him go." "Then we will take him," shot back the bristling Maeve.

And so begins the *Táin*, that epic story of the battle for the Brown Bull of Cooley. It is a story filled with passion and bravery, with greed and jealousy, a story of brotherly love, of honour and treachery, of courage and defeat, and a story laced with all manner of magical and fantastical happenings brought about by the Tuatha de Danaan, those powerful spirits of the other world.

Queen Maeve pits the full might of her army against a single foe, the young warrior Cuchulainn, defender of Ulster and her Brown Bull of Cooley. But Cuchulainn is watched over and protected by the good forces of the spirit world and his magical slingshot drives back Maeve and her army again and again. Following many days of fierce fighting, Cuchulainn is mortally wounded. He beseeches his faithful charioteer, Laeg, to strap him to a giant boulder so that Maeve and her army can see him on his feet. And as he is dying, the forces of King Conor and the fighting men of Ulster ride in to rout the warriors of Queen Maeve. She retreats, but not before she has succeeded in capturing the Brown Bull of Cooley.

Upon returning to Cruachan, Queen Maeve parades her prize animal in front of the astonished Ailill. "Now I am the wealthiest person in all Ireland," she boasts. And with that, the Brown Bull of Cooley turns on the prize animal, Finnbeannach, and tramples him into the ground. As Finnbeannach lies dead before his master, who is now trembling with fury, Ailill draws his sword. "I'll kill that cursed animal of yours," he roars. But as he advances on the animal, the magnificent Brown Bull of Cooley bellows and charges. Maeve and Ailill run for their lives. The Brown Bull scatters all before him, then turns and bolts for the hills — for the hills of Cooley and his true home in Ulster. Good triumphs over evil and so ends the epic story of the *Táin*.

We had reached the top of the mountain and there in quiet solitude rested the high cairn of Queen Maeve. Following in the tradition of all those who had gone before us, we each searched for a special stone to place on top of this massive mound of rocks. With a soft breeze licking our faces, a gentle mist rolling in from the sea and the evening's dusk drawing in, the spirits of Queen Maeve, Cuchulainn and the Tuatha de Danaan settled in around us. We would secretly take them home from this mystical place to the tumultuous concrete world of the South Bronx.

ೞ

A WEATHERED AND WORN *Naomh Éanna* took us on a three-hour journey from Galway City out into the Atlantic, her stormy seas pitching the ageing ferry about like a cork on the water. From the pier of Inis Mór, we lugged our scant belongings onto a fishing *curragh* and if we had suffered seasickness on the ferry, well this was to be the daddy of them all. Towering waves caught the little craft by the throat and hurled it into the air where it lay suspended in flight for several seconds. Then it crashed down into the roaring surf and was met by the next series of waves, just waiting to pitch it back into space. We clung onto the sides of the *curragh* and onto one another for dear life, drenched to the skin by the raging force of the ocean. We were heading for the middle of the three Aran Islands, the one that didn't have a pier and couldn't receive the ferry. We had no hope that we would ever make it.

The two island fishermen battled on, rowing furiously, catching wave after wave and steadying the craft with masterful skill. But we didn't know that. We thought they were plain crazy, taking us out into this gale. I couldn't swim and there were no life jackets on the *curragh*. My heart had leapt up into my throat and was choking me. It's a miracle it didn't just stop with fright. But eventually, after what seemed like an eternity, the little boat crashed onto shore. I had been so terrified that I had glued my eyes shut and only the jolt of the landing brought me back to my senses.

We peeled ourselves out of the *curragh* and stumbled up onto the rocky beach where Ruairi Ó Fathairte, titular head of the island, was waiting to greet us. There he stood, craggy face under a spray of black hair, wearing a blue woollen jacket and woollen pants with a pair of rough leather *pampooties* on his feet. There was only one other stranger on the island, an American university student called Ann, who was also living with Ruairi's family and was there to learn the Irish language.

Ruairi slung our sopping wet bags over his shoulder and led the way. He had enough English to be getting on with and informed us that we were now to become part of his family. His house was the biggest on the island, a two-storey rambling structure overlooking the shore. A concrete wall encircled the house and we were greeted every morning with the sight of Ruairi's six little sons sitting astride the wall, oars to hand, practising their strokes, their swaying bodies flowing effortlessly with the rhythm of the sea. They would be called to that sea soon enough and we were dumbfounded to hear that none of the islanders had ever learned to swim. Survival lay in man's command of the *curragh*, not in his attempt to conquer the wild forces of nature. That was then, but times have changed.

Daytime rambles to a collection of rocks overlooking the Atlantic, known locally as Synge's Chair, became our daily obsession. There we would sit, full of rapt attention and concentration, gazing out onto the horizon, trying to penetrate the mystery that had led John Millington Synge to his point of inspired genius. Another *Riders to the Sea* lurked somewhere deep within our consciousness. All we had to do was wait patiently and concentrate fiercely. This new Irish masterpiece would then rise to the surface, as predictably as day followed night. Of this, we were in no doubt. And Ellie wasn't even with us.

But as members of the Ó Fathairte household, we now had our daily chores. Land had to be made. The island was a mound of brittle stone. Islanders lived by fishing and knitting. All other supplies had to be brought over from Galway by ferry. One day, as we gathered on the shoreline waiting for the *Naomh Éanna* to drop anchor far out in the ocean, we clapped eyes on an unbelievable sight. Two big bullocks were being lowered by winches into the ocean. They were then fastened to two fragile *curraghs* and tugged ashore, the bewildered looking cattle floating above the crest of the water like inflated toys. All we could think about was the once-mighty Finnbeannach lying dead before his master and the Brown Bull of Cooley charging off into the sunset. Perhaps the offspring of his offspring's offspring were coming back to restore the magnificence of Queen Maeve's lost kingdom. This could be the very start.

The real toys came later: keg after keg of prime Guinness to fuel the island's *síbín*.

Our job was to collect the tons of slippery, slimy seaweed that littered the shoreline and then pack it into the wicker baskets that straddled the backs of the island's few donkeys. Then we led the animals back up to the house, unloaded the seaweed and returned to the shoreline for similar baskets of sand. This procedure was repeated over and over until Ruairí called a halt. He would then mix the seaweed and sand, breaking the mixture down into a fine pulp, and in this fashion, land for planting was made. Seaweed was also cooked and used as a sweet for after dinner. It was called *duilse* and we added that to our list of culinary disasters. We hated it.

Every evening, as light began to fade over this rugged little world anchored precariously in mid-ocean, a familiar ritual would commence. All the unmarried young men and women on the island would begin to saunter along the only path that led down to a large flat rock that stood at the point on the beach where the fishing *curraghs* were moored. This particular rock was at least ten feet by twelve feet and the surface was as smooth as glass, polished as it was by the slip and slide of so many dancing feet over so many years. Men sat along one side of the rock with women along the other. An accordion player, a few fiddlers and a tin whistler were at the head. When everyone was seated cross-legged on the rock, the dance could begin.

The young men would rise, cross the dance rock, and formally ask each woman to dance. *"Ar mhaith leat damhsa, le do thoil?"* to which the answer was, *"'Sea, go raibh maith agat."* To refuse the offer of a dance would have been considered the height of ignorance and a display of gauche behaviour the likes of which would not be tolerated in any civilised society. It just did not happen.

Fast and furious spins around the floor marked the progression of county sets; the Kerry Set followed by the Clare Set, the Leitrim Set, the Cavan Set and then when energy began to flag, the half-sets. Fortunately, we were as accomplished at the intricacies of set-dancing as any native-born and could stomp and batter with the best of them. Pauses in the dance were punctuated by the chilling sound of a *sean nós* voice rising from some dark corner of the gathering, never announced, but knowingly expected by all. That mournful sound sent shivers up my spine, sitting there in the open air under a moonlit sky, amidst people who knew only that we were, like so many of their own, from the next parish across the Atlantic.

The return home was every bit as enchanting as the whole evening put together. The men would lead the way up the dark incline, talking quietly together, the muted hum of their deep voices stirring the night. They were followed by a procession of chattering women bringing up the rear. This procession rambled away all around the island, dropping each and every woman off at her own house, until the last female was seen safely home. The men would then retire to the island *síbín* for their nightly libations.

Our libations were waiting for us in the Ó Fathairte's kitchen. Three candles, each in a proper candlestick, sat beside a box of Patterson's Friendly Matches. When we had lit the candles, we were then able to pour the hot cocoa that had been prepared ear-lier and kept warm in a large glass thermos. Our repast was com-plete with a plateful of Jacob's Mariettas. Like the Victorians of old, we in 1950s Inis Meáin made our way upstairs and into bed by candlelight.

Cʒ

OUR LAST STOP ON THAT FIRST TRIP to Ireland was to the Taaffe stronghold in Banteer, the scene of so many painful memories for both Mom and Dad. But we were unaware of the intrigues of fam-ily history at the time. We were visiting Mom's family — Uncle Jack, Aunt Hannie and all our cousins — the legendary Taaffes.

Little had changed since Mom and Dad had left, more than twenty years before. We had heard stories about hiding from the Black and Tans under McCarthy's Bridge so often, we recognised the spot on sight.

Aunt Hannie's one-bedroomed stone cottage sat nestled among a clump of trees set far back from the road. It was to this house that all those American parcels that our Mom had sent, for years and years, had come. (And it was to this house that our sis-ter, Ellie, would continue to send parcels in the years to come, but they would then be coming from her new home in Dublin and not from the USA.)

Hannie's two daughters, Bridie and Kathleen, were living at home, along with their brother Timothy. As we sat down to tea we discovered that Hannie possessed a rare and wonderful gift. She could read the leaves.

And so began another rite of passage, another mystical link with that other world. Hannie boiled water in a black kettle that sung above a smouldering turf fire. She then took down a yellow-ing ceramic teapot from the wooden ledge above the fireplace and scalded the inside of the pot with the boiling water. After swish-ing the water about inside for a minute or two, she emptied the pot outside the front door. Then she took down a small package of

Lyon's Tea and carefully measured out the dark black leaves, one teaspoon for each of us and one for the pot. She filled the pot with boiling water and covered it with a well worn, hand-knitted tea cosy. The teapot with its little bobbing hat sat in the middle of the table like a pot-bellied baby doll. Hannie placed her two hands around the teapot and waited.

The cottage was dimly lit with a single bulb and though the sun was shining brightly outdoors, we sat around the highly scrubbed wooden table in near darkness. At last, when Hannie was satisfied that the tea had satisfactorily drawn, she poured. What came out was so dark and so strong you could trot a horse across it. We added a drop of milk each but there was no sugar. Then we drank this hot, bitter, stomach-churning offering down to the last drop. We had to, because we desperately wanted our leaves to be read.

We were mesmerised as we watched this dark and wiry little woman, who was our Mom's sister, lift one cup after another to scrutinise the cluster of leaves that clung to their insides. I heard nothing she had to say to any of the others in the room, so riveted was I on what might transpire when my turn arrived. When it did, my heart just about leapt out of my mouth.

"You will soon cross water," said Hannie. And I waited. That was no surprise. Wouldn't I soon be going home?

"And you will cross water scores of times more in a long life. I see a sandy-haired youth with whom you will have two daughters, maybe more. There will be storms and many clouds and some sunshine. I see many strangers, but I don't know what that means."

This was just a bit of fun. Right? But there was something haunting about Hannie that touched us. Nobody giggled. Nobody laughed. When she began to clear away the tea things, we quietly rose to take our leave for our Uncle Jack's house. Hannie smiled and called *"Beannacht Dé libh"*, as she wished us a safe journey to the Bronx and a speedy return "home". One insipidly limp little teabag floating about in a lukewarm cup of water would never again be the same.

When we entered Healy's Pub at the crossroads, in the company of Uncle Jack, we were instantly recognised as Nellie's children. Our cousin, Sean Taaffe, was probably the most handsome man we had met in Ireland and Aunt Hannie, the kindest. Trees were now growing through the roof of Mom and Dad's old home and we dug up a rose bush to bring back to the Bronx. It was eventually planted under the gentle figures of Romeo and Juliet, and like all other transplants from the Rebel County, it survived. The lurch back from the enchantment of Aran to the concrete jungles of New York was more traumatic.

CB

Chapter 5

FORT APACHE

THE MELLOW SERENITY of the post-war fifties was giving way to a new social turbulence in the United States. A decade of the rebellious sixties was on the horizon and with it dope rocketed into our world. It didn't creep in slowly and insidiously, gradually insinuating itself into our lives. Dope arrived without warning and with a massive kick. One day, we were innocently on the street playing Ring-a-Levio and the next, our friends were skulking around the markets with vacant, blood-shot eyes or stumbling into alleys to drag on joints or shoot up on horse.

There were two ways to go and the choice was stark. We could hang on to the old ways of our parents, our schools and our church, and with the help of God, move up and out or we could cave in and run with the crowd. "Without a shadow of doubt, the end of that line will be prison bars or an early grave," warned Mom and Dad as they watched with sad eyes as young Richie Mahoney was transformed from a healthy, happy teenager into a furtive, shambling wreck.

Richie had been the brightest star in the firmament, the whiz-kid of St Jerome's. "Now, God help him, he haunts the dregs of humanity, lurking around the subway station, picking pockets and running in the shadows. It wasn't for this he was born." Poor Mom, her heart broke every time she passed him, propped up against the subway railings, bone-thin with sunken eyes and crusted lips. But to her, he was the same ten-year-old Richie, sweeping our kitchen floor because he loved our Mom and she loved him.

Drugs were flooding our neighbourhood at such a ferocious clip that pitched battles in a rapidly escalating drugs wars were being fought out nightly in the middle of our street. The Good Humour man, in his crisp white uniform, continued to push his ice-cream cart down the street, but what he was selling had little to do with popsicles. Under the watchful eye of our Dad, we became educated in the street culture of drugs.

Gone were the easy days of carefree innocence. A telephone was urgently installed in our house and we were warned not to attempt to walk home unaccompanied after dark. We were cautioned to ring the house first and then wait for Dad, or one of our *greenhorns*, to come and meet us at Brook Avenue. High school outings had to be planned and timed and deadlines met with rigidity. Life became fraught and scary. Homemade zip-guns were the street weapons of choice and our once-cosy neighbourhood became notoriously known throughout New York as Fort Apache. The death toll from fatal shootings, brutal stabbings and drugs overdoses reached epidemic proportions. And Father Michael Crowley, a newly ordained missionary priest from Clonakilty, County Cork came into our lives.

I don't suppose Father Crowley ever really knew what an impact he had on us. We were gangs of very raw, very untutored youth running wild on the streets of the Bronx. Our parents were all from the old country, wherever that might be, bewildered and angered by the rapidity of change surging all around them but helpless to hold it back. They had invested their lives in this American Dream and suddenly, without warning, it had imploded. Their lives, their homes, their children were all under attack from elements they knew nothing about.

That was then, when the evil enemy was drugs. The enemy was coming from outside our borders but trafficking was being fuelled by greed from within. New York City was the enemy's target. The Bronx, with its rapidly changing social and cultural make-up, was in the front line.

Father Crowley decided that what St Jerome's Parish needed was a youth club and his announcement from the pulpit one Sunday morning was met with a level of derision normally reserved for the reviled Rockefellers. Heroin and hash were being flogged openly on the streets like cotton candy and Father Crowley's Saturday Night Hops were going to counter that?

Cʙ

BUT THOSE PARENTS DIDN'T KNOW about Father's secret weapon, sixteen-year-old Eleanor O'Connell.

The annual St Patrick's Day concert in the school auditorium had so far survived the changing cultural climate. This was the premier showcase for BIC talent. Aspiring showmen, with dubious names like Maldonado and Rivera became Irish for the night and joined a long list of hopefuls auditioning for a spot. Talent was not limited but time was. So only the very best got on the bill.

Young Bobby White, a brilliant tenor and son of a noted radio broadcaster, was the local hero. He was a regular performer at Carnegie Hall and he had even appeared on the Ed Sullivan TV Show. With an elegant home on Alexander Avenue, the Whites ranked high up among the Bronx gentry. Bobby would take the stage with a whimsical rendition of "The Low Back Car", skilfully playing his audience and wrapping them around his fingers. He would then follow up with something like "Sweet Peggy O'Neill", encouraging his audience to sing along. But his final offering of "Danny Boy" was the *coup de grace*. After that, nobody would be left in any doubt about who was the star of this show!

Several years younger, and with an untrained voice, Eleanor would then step up to the mike. She was on home ground. She commanded the stage with a presence that intimidated the hardest of men and her fragile frame masked a voice with timbre and tone that made grown men weep. The audience disappeared and she was in a world of her own, transported somewhere up there where angels tread.

Father Crowley was captivated. The Saturday Night Hops were going down a storm, but now he had another idea. He would turn Eleanor loose and let her stage a show of her own. He had no doubt she could do it. And she needed no convincing.

The show was titled "Top Hat", produced, directed by and starring Eleanor O'Connell. She commandeered every piece of stage furniture, equipment, scenery and lighting as well as every costume needed from the shops, markets, schools and churches in the vicinity. She pulled together a rag-a-tag army of near-delinquents and beat rhythm and song into them. She brooked no dissent. She demanded full respect and she got it. And she was sixteen years of age.

"Top Hat" opened in St Jerome's Auditorium to a packed house. We sang and danced and tripped across the stage like veterans, keeping an ever-watchful eye on Eleanor, who remained waiting in the wings until her number was announced. And what burst onto the stage was a revelation. During clandestine visits downtown, Ellie had ventured farther south than usual — into the unknown and risqué territory of Greenwich Village where Modern Dance was all the craze. Eleanor had inveigled her way into several dance classes and now she exploded onto St Jerome's stage as Isadora Duncan, a writhing, squirming, leaping contortion of movement. Somewhere beneath this swirling sea of scarves was a sixteen-year old girl with no training but with all the confidence of a tsarina. The audience was dumbstruck. They had been swept along from, "Struttin' out with my baby . . . in my black hat and my bow tie and my tails . . ." to this volcanic eruption in the space of seconds. For the first time in her performing life, Ellie didn't sing. She had found a new challenge, the first of many.

All New York City minors were entitled to apply for working papers at the age of fourteen and this we did with an almost religious zeal. On our fourteenth birthday, we would take the Third

Avenue "El" to the Labour Relations Office on Tremont Avenue, produce our birth certificates and receive our passports to the working world. Next stop would be Woolworth's Five and Ten on 138th Street or a McCreery's somewhere downtown. The idea was to get after-school and Saturday work in order to pay for our subway fares to high school and our school uniforms and supplies. Our sister, Ellie's, pay went elsewhere.

Eleanor was now a teenager at Cathedral High School in Manhattan where her fascination for the world of music and cinema blossomed into a total obsession. Schoolwork was simply not on the agenda. She dismissed it with haughty disdain and a lacerating tongue, deliberately choosing to cut classes and haunt the movie houses along 42nd Street with her co-conspirator, Gina Gangi. Gina was just as enraptured with the glittering lights of Broadway as Ellie. They went to school together, cut school together, worked after school together and fed each other's hunger for the celluloid screen.

Mom was certainly aware of Ellie's extracurricular activities because she faithfully attended every parent conference ever held. But she kept the information back from Dad, knowing full well what the consequences would be; there would be "wigs on the green" and holy war declared. Ellie would be grounded, long before that particular idea became fashionable. Mom was wise enough to know that trying to ground Ellie would be like trying to hold back a raging storm.

It was while prowling the Great White Way with her trusted cohort, Gina, that Eleanor came upon the Dramatic Workshop directed by Saul Colin. Eleanor was still in school, no more than seventeen years of age, when she auditioned for a place and was accepted.

This was the inner sanctum of American theatre and it numbered among its illustrious alumni Harry Belafonte, Marlon Brando, Ben Gazzara, Shelley Winters, Elaine Stritch, Rod Steiger, Tennessee Williams, Bea Arthur and Walter Matthau. Even in the far corners of the South Bronx, these were household names. And now Eleanor O'Connell was to become one of them.

Miraculously, and without any visible effort at all, she managed to complete high school and graduate with a respectable academic diploma. And then she threw herself headlong into dramatic studies.

In order to finance her studies, Ellie took a job as night receptionist in a Greenwich Village hotel. And Mom nearly lost her reason. The thought of Ellie riding alone on the subway at some ungodly hour of the morning, then walking from the subway to the house in a lawless neighbourhood put the heart across her. So it was agreed that Ellie would stay at the hotel at least until daybreak. Nonetheless, for several years, Mom spent many a sleepless night waiting for the key in the door, waiting for Ellie to be safely home.

It was far from Broadway that Mom was born, but apart from worrying about her safety, neither she nor Dad ever tried to influence Ellie's hopes and dreams. And when Ellie began to appear in Dr Colin's theatre productions, Mom was right there in the audience, bewildered but proud. "Welcome, Mrs McGillicuddy," he would say in his cultivated continental accent, bestowing a chivalrous kiss on her cheek as she entered his darkened auditorium. Mom was Irish and McGillicuddy was the most Irish-sounding name that Dr Colin knew. He loved it. He bestowed it on Mom, along with the chivalrous kiss and a congratulatory plea: "You have a delightful and brilliant young daughter. Cherish her!"

❦

KEVIN HAD, BY THIS TIME, completed his two-year tour of duty with the American Army and had returned home to join the New York City Police Department. He was immediately posted to the newly formed 41st Precinct Narcotics Squad and one of his first arrests was that of Richie Mahoney, now big-time drugs dealer. Kevin's evidence at trial put Richie away in the Federal Penitentiary in Kentucky for a very long time and it nearly finished Kevin's fledging career. He was shattered. He had been responsible for arresting and convicting a childhood friend, one close enough to have been a brother. Divided loyalties are a heavy burden to carry.

Kevin had always been solid and steady and the golden boy with the female members of our extended family. He was the very essence of an O'Connell in appearance, tall with sandy blond, curly hair and blue eyes. But by nature, he should have been Timothy O'Connell's son, and not Michael's. As Kevin grew from boy to man and as he began to form his own political and social opinions, father and son began to clash.

Kevin had taken to United States military training like the proverbial duck to water and, in the transition, he had become one hundred per cent American. He was the original straight arrow. He supported the ultra-conservative John Birch Society, railed against creeping Communism, defended the controversial Catholic priest, Father Coughlan and joined the Republican Party. Dad remained an obdurate defender of unions and working men's rights, loathed and detested Senator Joe McCarthy and creeping consumerism, was a confirmed anti-cleric and had mellowed enough to finally vote for the Democratic Party. Consequently, our house turned into a verbal battlefield with Mom trying to keep the warring sides apart.

So deep was Catholic Irish American attachment to the Democratic Party that a story our cousin, Johnny Ferreira, tells about two old Irishmen meeting on the streets of the old neighbourhood one Sunday afternoon illustrates it all.

Mick was all a-fluster as he greeted his friend, Jimmy, outside the Leitrim House, ducking his head sideways and muttering conspiratorially out of the side of his mouth. "There's terrible news about McGinty," he intoned, sucking in his breath and drawing deeply on his chewed-up pipe. "Terrible, just terrible!"

"What's happened, man," rushed in his friend, thinking the worst. "Has he died?"

"Oh, Jaysus, no! It's shockin' awful. Worse. Much worse than that! McGinty's after joining the Republican Party."

"Ah, for Jaysus' sake. Cop yourself on, man," roared Mick, wheeling on his heels and jabbing poor old Jimmy in the chest. "Where ever did you get the likes of that? It's lies. Damn lies! Amn't I only after seeing him this morning at the nine o'clock mass!"

But regular mass-going did little to defuse the explosive situation that was rapidly developing under our roof. Kevin valiantly defended the Republican Party's political values, citing story after story of widespread corruption within the Democratic Party machine. "Listen here, fella," retorted Dad, after listening to one such treacherous tirade, "the only difference between Democratic corruption and Republican corruption is that with the Democrats, a little of it trickles down to the likes of us!"

The divided political loyalties of a previous generation, from another land, had come home to roost in the Bronx.

Emmett slipped through this maelstrom of unleashed emotion with relative ease. He was a Taaffe and well endowed with all the Taaffe cunning and charm. In the midst of all this heavy-duty politicking, Emmett had become a minor celebrity. Geographically, he had moved in the opposite direction to Ellie, uptown instead of downtown, and joined the Fordham Roller-Skating Club. Emmett began to appear in the local papers, resplendent in satin and sequins, coolly pitching his dazzling dance-skating partner into a mid-air spin. In the middle of a knock-down, no-holds-barred battle of words between Kevin and Dad, Emmett would appear flashing a new golden trophy. Kevin would retreat to bed, verbally bruised and bloodied, while Emmett would saunter off with the mild admonition to "tell your story walking".

And smugly abscond he would, untouched by the domestic turmoil whirling around him. For there was another aspect to

Emmett's charmed life. His bedroom was papered with flow charts gleaned from the Wall Street Journal. Unknown to all but himself, Emmett was a budding financial wizard. He barely scraped through high school and hadn't yet bothered to enrol in college, but he was becoming a competent engineer's draughtsman and in whatever time he could spare from the glittering world of national roller-blading, and the more pedestrian world of making a living, he invested in studying the Wall Street Stock Market.

ᑕᑐ

I FELL SOMEWHERE IN THE MIDDLE of all this; self-sufficient and studious. I simply loved books. I loved the smell of them, the feel of them, the rustle of pages and the intriguing patterns that words made as they flowed across the page. I loved writing, its physical movement and the careful formation of letters. I loved the Mott Haven Library and its solitary solace. In the hush of its book-lined aisles, I discovered a world far beyond the South Bronx and I wanted to explore every tantalising inch of it.

Mother Mary Ruth was the principal of St Jerome's Parochial School. She was a formidable figure in flowing folds of black that rustled softly as she swept along the school corridors. A startling white wimple encased her face so tightly that not a trace of hair could be seen and we spent hours speculating on whether or not she had any hair at all. The common wisdom was that her head was shaved. A stiffly starched white bib encircled her chest from shoulder to shoulder. We would watch entranced as she burrowed beneath the rippling folds of her habit to produce rosary beads, handkerchiefs, fountain pens, safety pins, band-aids, prayer books and note-pads. Mother Mary Ruth was a walking bundle of mysteries.

This formidable lady kept all of her students in her sights and she found places in Catholic high schools for as many graduating eighth graders as she could. Within the New York City School System, there were two choices. One could attend a public school, which provided free education to everyone, or choose a fee-paying religious-based school. The Jewish community ran Yeshivas for their young male students while Catholic boys and girls headed for Catholic High Schools. But it was an expensive proposition and one that not every family could afford.

That's where Mother Mary Ruth came in. She investigated every possibility, knowing which entrance exams suited her students best and making sure we were all primed and ready and in with a chance for a scholarship. That was the only way many of us could hope to get a good high school education. She was a woman with a mission.

My high school became St Jean Baptiste on East 75th Street, in the heart of affluent Manhattan. St Jean's was a highly rated and expensive girls' academy to which I had won a partial scholarship. If I were to accept the offer, my parents would need to come up with the balance of the monthly tuition. At the time, there were three of us attending fee-paying Catholic high schools. In addition to that, there were all the music and dancing lessons. Dad carried on with his two jobs while the rest of us got after-school work to help with the cost. How Mom and Dad managed to pull it all off without robbing banks is the second greatest mystery of all time.

My working papers led me to Stern's Department Store on 42nd Street, right across from the New York City Public Library with its massive roaring lions mounted high on stone plinths, poised and ready to protect the treasures within. I worked at the hosiery counter in the Bargain Basement, selling second-rate goods to a grumbling public. "Second-Hand Rose", that was me. But it never bothered me. I was there for one reason only; to keep me in that top-class girls' academy.

I always knew that I would go to college, whatever it might take to get me there. But college was still not the norm for girls. Most of my friends were either engaged to be married before leaving high school, going into the convent or heading for work in the New York City Telephone Company. None of that was for me. I loved learning. I had no idea what I wanted to be or do but I wanted desperately to stay in school.

My English teacher at St Jean's, Miss Mangan, looked to me like she was dressed by the editors of *Seventeen* magazine, that fashion bible of American teenage girls. She had long blonde hair that turned under in a gentle pageboy and she wore soft lambs' wool sweaters with pleated plaid skirts. To me, she was pure magic.

Every Friday afternoon we got to put our heads down on our desks, close our eyes and listen as Miss Mangan's quirky, clipped midwest voice drifted out over the hushed classroom. She would be reading choice extracts from the great American classics. My heart bled for the tortured but brave Hester Prynne with her blazing Scarlet Letter on her breast, and it danced with the glorious Hiawatha on the shores of Gitchee Gumee. But we only got snatches of the real thing, just enough to fit into a forty-five-minute class period and whet our appetites for more.

Then that same Miss Mangan came up with an extraordinary idea. She thought that I should apply for admission to her old Alma Mater, the University of Michigan at Ann Arbor. I was dumbfounded. Warsaw, Munich, Russia, Sicily, Belfast, Kerry — those I could handle. All very familiar and non-threatening. But Ann Arbor, Michigan! I had never heard of the place. How on earth would I get there? What would I do there? Where would I live? How would I ever get back? I was almost overwhelmed by the idea. She might as well have suggested that I go to college on the moon!

Ann Arbor, Michigan was never going to be a runner. Going away to college was for the rich and famous, the thing of dreams, and I was wise enough to know that my dreams would have to be fulfilled much closer to home.

So I sat every entrance exam that came my way and once again I was offered a partial scholarship. This time it was to Marymount College on East 72nd Street in Manhattan.

ᘓ

MARYMOUNT COLLEGE FOR WOMEN was about as fashionable and elite an institution as one could find. Its student body was drawn from New York Society with addresses on Park and Fifth Avenues. A small number of academic scholarships were reserved for talented youth, and strangely enough, these usually had addresses in Upper Manhattan and the South Bronx.

At the outset of my studies, I was deliriously happy. I was in college. I had to do a full year of core courses, including maths, history, literature, philosophy and science before deciding on a major area of study. But this suited me down to the ground, except for one dark spot. Everyone had to do Speech. This was long before regional accents became acceptable and we were all expected to conform to the standard. Changing my accent was not part of my long-term plan.

But there was a much greater obstacle than my accent on the horizon. Ellie and Gretta were now in Catholic high schools and needed looking after. My college expenses could seriously drain limited resources. So I now had to work every night at Stern's Department Store in order to make up the balance of my tuition. But this after-school working very soon brought me into serious conflict with the Dean of Students.

All Marymount women were expected to take an active part in extracurricular activities, thus demonstrating true school spirit. Total commitment to the annual college "Sing" was the absolute minimum required.

"Sing" was an intra-mural competition among the four college years, from Freshmen through to Seniors. At the beginning of the fall term, a theme was decided upon by each of the years and preparation and practice that would do justice to a full Broadway show would begin. Because of the highly selective nature of college admission, a large proportion of the Marymount student body were, at the very least, musically and artistically proficient, with a glimmer of real talent breaking through. So the finished product was always scintillatingly professional. But talent aside, time was the true test of class spirit.

And time was the very thing I had so little of. As soon as my last class finished, I was out the door and onto the subway, heading downtown to my bargain basement. Such blatant disregard for my collegiate responsibilities did not sit very well with Mother Superior. After having absented myself from several of the initial rehearsals, I was summoned to the Dean's Office.

"My dear child," she intoned, brimming with benign concern, "You truly disappoint me. You have been offered the most wonderful opportunity. To study at Marymount College, to have all of New York City as your campus is not something to be taken lightly. If you apply yourself to all aspects of your college life, you will leave us a very accomplished young lady indeed. But you have, until now, shown a shocking disregard for the benevolence shown to you. You will, from here on out, attend and participate fully in all 'Sing' rehearsals and show the kind of school spirit we expect from all our girls."

"Well, hold on just a little minute now. What planet do you live on?" I wondered to myself, as I tried to draw in the breath that had just been knocked out of me and steady myself. "If this woman isn't smart enough to understand that I have to work to go to college, she's going to find out right now."

"Sister, do you know where I live?" I asked, with all the respect I could muster. "I come from the Bronx, from a place called Fort Apache. But don't think I'm poor. I was never poor. I just don't have any money. And I need money to come to your college. So I work after school. And I'll keep right on working until the end of the year and then you won't have to concern yourself about me any more because I won't be coming back."

I excused myself and left her office shaking with rage. "She thinks she can make me bow and scrape because she's let me come to her snobby school? Well I didn't come here to learn how to set a formal table and she's damn well not going to change my accent, no matter how hard she tries." I'd figure something out. I just didn't quite know what.

I didn't go to any "Sing" rehearsals and she didn't bother me again. But my grades became a disaster. I couldn't rise above a "C" in anything, me, a solid Grade "A" student all my life. That nearly sent me into orbit. I knew I was better than that but I'd never make the grade at Marymount. It was nobody's fault. We were just an ill-fit. I'd try Notre Dame. That's what I'd do.

There is a certain resilience and maybe a lot of not knowing any better that comes with our sort of upbringing. I was barely seventeen when I started college and I made all of the decisions about my life myself. My parents worked hard and taught us well. They gave us every chance they could. They watched over us and kept us safe. But they didn't know this new world of college, theatre and high finance. They trusted us, after they had done all they could, to do the right thing for ourselves.

Notre Dame College was run under the auspices of the Congregation of Notre Dame and the order's nuns were addressed as Mother. I rang up the Registrar of Notre Dame College and asked for an appointment. I took the subway to Battery Park, walked a few blocks, past the chapel built with contributions from Irish domestic servants, and then took the ferry to Staten Island. Finally, a short bus ride took me to the top of Grymes Hill and from there, the highest point on the East Coast between New York State and Florida, I gazed out on one of the most awesome sights I had ever seen. New York Bay sprawled out before me with ocean freighters, luxury liners and spunky little tugboats sailing by. Lady Liberty and her lighted torch of freedom stood out in regal relief. The towers of New York City's majestic skyline glistened in the morning sun, an eternal magnet for the tired and worn, the shackled and oppressed, all those longing to be free.

The Dean of Admissions seemed a little taken aback that I had come alone. She had expected my parents to accompany me. Parents, the decision-makers and fee payers, were the norm. But that initial little discomfort became more exacerbated as I set about explaining the reason for my visit. What I needed was a transfer of my scholarship from Marymount to Notre Dame. It was as simple as that. And when I wasn't asked to leave immediately, well, I took that as a good sign.

The Dean seemed a bit confused, "Tell me, Geraldine, why do you want to leave Marymount? It is an excellent college with an excellent reputation and, furthermore, it is so much nearer to where you live. It will take you the best part of four hours to make this journey back and forth every day."

This was my moment of truth and there was no point in trying to hide anything.

"Well, Mother, there are a lot of reasons. But I really don't think I'm getting a fair shake over there. I have no interest in doing etiquette and diction classes, I'm not supposed to work after school, and my grades have fallen through the floor. I just know that I would do a whole lot better over here."

Then we got down to the nitty-gritty. "We can't just transfer a scholarship, Geraldine. Marymount awarded that and it's not transferable. But leave your transcript with me, and your high school records, and let me think about this. I'll be in touch."

She was true to her word and got back to me within the month. She could offer me a grant, not a scholarship, which meant that I would have to work in the cafeteria or in the admissions office several hours a day. The grant would be equal to my former scholarship. And she had no objection to me working after school as long as I kept my grade point average up. It was a good deal. I took it.

CB

BUT LIFE WAS BECOMING INTOLERABLE around East 139th Street. Not alone had the drugs scourge shot out of control but the whole ethnic make-up of the neighbourhood was changing. Unknown cultures with strange beliefs were beginning to invade our once congenial society.

Panicky parents began to flee to the safety of suburban America. And in their place came a new wave of immigrants, this time from the Caribbean Islands of Puerto Rico, the Dominican Republic and Cuba. The easy camaraderie of European immigrants vanished and in its place came a fractious relationship filled with suspicion and fear.

The new arrivals were from tropical islands with a culture and language completely alien to the rest of us. And where past immigrants had struggled to learn and use English, and had often massacred it in the process, the new arrivals, though coming from different islands, spoke the same language. Learning English to survive was not as critical as it had once been. They were able to hold onto their own language and function in their own language and this made ordinary social activity with the earlier immigrants much more difficult.

Bongo drums began to take the place of accordions and fiddles while jigs and reels were replaced with the cha-cha-cha. Irish potatoes disappeared when green bananas came onto the grocery shelves. The Casino Cinema became the Teatro Puerto Rico and the Star of Munster fell to the Latin-American Ballroom.

The Kellys were among the first wave to depart for the gentrified green spaces of Westchester County. They were soon followed by the O'Donnells, who moved to Yonkers, and the Corcorans to Throggs Neck. But stubbornly, Dad held on. He refused to be "forced out" of his home. And this intractable stubbornness of Dad's began to sow seeds of discord within the family at large.

"What exactly do they think they are doing, living in a lawless land?" asked the relatives, harboured as they were in the safe environs of Brooklyn and Queens. Mom was under constant pressure to move — for safety's sake. We, the South Bronx Five, began to be seen as victims of an eccentric man — a flaming socialist in a galloping capitalist society. *The Daily Worker* was his newspaper of choice while the *New York Herald Tribune* was a "yellow rag" from the corrupt Hearst newspaper empire. He was a man out of step with the political and social mores of his time and he paid a heavy price for his principles. He was an outlaw among conservative Irish-America but, in his mind, he was still the "Keeper of the Flame".

But Dad was not alone in his defence of our neighbourhood. Mom had lived in the South Bronx for twenty-eight years. She knew every street intimately and had friends and relations all around her. She knew all the shopkeepers by name and they all knew her. St Jerome's Parish was at the centre of her world.

Mothers didn't babysit friends' children in those days; they cared for them as part of their family. The lives of all the children we grew up with were Mom's life. She cheered with them in good times and she suffered with them when things went wrong. Everyone loved her.

And even when the neighbourhood started to change, and strange and frightening influences started seeping in, Mom defended her ground.

When the Kellys left, a Puerto Rican family moved in beside us and we settled down to fairly normal neighbourly relations with Pee Wee Morales, the head of house. Until one day, while Dad was sitting on the stoop, he witnessed a clandestine transaction going on through the barred windows in the aireyway. That was too close for comfort. It was definitely time to go.

We moved to the very respectable area of Parkchester, still in the Bronx but now on the tree-lined streets of "uptown". But Mom never really settled in. She pined for her old life, her old neighbours and friends, the soothing comfort of the familiar. And when Aunt Mollie and family left for Rochester, in upstate New York, the final pillars of Mom's world came tumbling down. Her family circle was becoming smaller and smaller and moving much farther away.

Kevin had met and married Kathy Nolan, a greenhorn from County Roscommon, and they moved upstate to Rockland County, a safe haven for young families. The first grandchildren began to make their appearances: Liam, Kevin Michael, Sean and Tara.

Meanwhile, Emmett had spread his wings and discovered the great US of A. First he headed south and from there it was off to the midwest. Then it was on to California dreaming, all the time doing college courses wherever he happened to land and dabbling more and more in the nomadic world of oil and finance. He began speaking a language more foreign to us than Greek — stocks and bond, highs and lows, indices and exchange rates. Dad seemed to be the only one with any clue what Emmett was on about. How did *he* find out about such things, we wondered?

Gretta had followed me on to St Jean's High School, quit trying to beat people up in the street and turned her attention to beating them in competition. She became a leading light in Irish dancing circles, having joined forces with The McNiffs, a charismatic and ground-breaking group of dancers from Belfast. Irish dancing in New York was never for the faint of heart; it has always been the Olympic sport of Irish-America and the world that spawned *Riverdance*.

There were punishing dancing practices several times a week in a downtown studio lined with floor-to-ceiling mirrors. Pulsating rhythms were drummed out on the wooden floor, with bodies leaping and swirling and feet hammering and battering and dancers collapsing at the end of it all in a lather of sweat. "Rally one, rally two, rally rally hop back. Rally rally hop back. Rally rally hop back. Hop one click your heel, hop two click your heel", with rocks and cross-keys and dizzying combinations of spins, slaps and stamps. The chat was all about leotards and costumes and hard shoes and soft shoes. Late-night sessions in the White Horse Inn of the East Village went on into the early hours of the morning, with ferocious debates raging about the merits of *Comhdháil* versus *Coimisiún*.

Because various forms of "splits" are part of Irish life, it was no surprise when even the relatively cultured world of Irish danc-

ing suffered a severe rupture. Those in the *Comhdháil* camp remained committed to the tradition of simple dress, rigid body,
still hands and a set pattern of foot movements. *Coimisiún* was
forward-looking, seeing Irish dance as a progressive art form,
open to change and development. The McNiffs had not yet nailed
their colours to a mast. So the beat went on, with more trips to Ireland and more voyages of discovery. But now Gretta travelled by
air to Belfast, packing dancing shoes instead of wooden crates.

og

GRYMES HILL IN THE AUTUMN of the year intoxicated me. Crimson
and orange leaves rustled and dropped, pirouetting in the breeze
before settling softly on the somnolent country lanes of Staten Island. The fruity odour of burning leaves and their friendly crackle
underfoot fed the fancies of my mind. As I rambled about Notre
Dame's college campus, breathing in its bittersweet smells, I began to construct a plan, an ambitious plan, to see the world — the
real world, not the world as seen in the pages of a book but the
world as seen through my own eyes.

Gretta had graduated from high school and was working in
Memorial Hospital in Manhattan and she became an eager col-
luder in the plan. I was doing a Political Science degree at Notre
Dame and working at Stern's Department Store in the evenings.
That and my in-house grant covered all my college expenses. But
if I wanted to see the world after graduation, I would have to do a
whole lot better than that. So I took on a reservations job with
American Airlines, working the midnight to 9.00 am shift on Friday and Saturday nights. The office was in the bustling theatre
district on West 45th Street, so I was safe to travel to work just as
the shows were letting out and safe to travel home as the city was
re-awakening. Every penny I saved from that job went into my
world travel fund.

Gretta and I were well on track, with two years of work ahead
and time to stash away our savings. All we needed were a couple

of willing accomplices to add spice to the adventure. And we found them without half trying. Kathy Morgan and Betty Magee, two of my classmates at Notre Dame, leapt aboard.

Then Emmett decided that we were not going without him. But he would only go as far as Dublin. We, the girls, would then be on our own.

My life at Notre Dame was crammed full of work and study, with me a willing and enthusiastic college club joiner. My earlier aversion to extracurricular activities dissipated rapidly once the compulsory social factor had disappeared. I joined the Literary Club, *Scoop*, the college newspaper, the Debating Society and the Student Council. And I relished every class, every paper and every wacky philosophy lecture delivered by the eccentric but brilliant Dr Seguin.

During our final college year, travel plans moved into high gear, with daily meetings held in the Staten Island Ferry Terminal, on the Staten Island Ferry, in the college café and coffee houses along the length and breadth of Broadway. We graduated in May and then the serious work began, every one of us putting in all the hours that God sent. D-Day was planned for October.

Lured by exuberant tales of our seafaring days aboard the *SS America*, Kathy and Betty demanded an ocean voyage and Gretta and I were only too happy to oblige. The *SS America* once again became our home for the five-day crossing from New York City to Cobh. What was to follow was a seriously bizarre three-month jaunt through Europe.

CB

"I DON'T THINK I'LL GO DOWN to breakfast this morning. I'm not very hungry," says Kathy as we dress and prepare for the coming day. Life aboard ship had been a whirlwind since the first blast of the ship's horn, as we steamed away and left New York Harbour in our wake. Our twenty-four-hour clock was now punctuated by *food!* Gone were the days of tea and a slice of toast on the run. Enter an army of charming, smiling waiters in their dazzling whites, with fetching little white towels draped nattily over their arms, skating around the dining room with only one goal — to please.

Kathy was a near anorexic, pencil-thin and able to live on warmed-up tea. But a funny thing happened to her on the way to Europe. She developed an appetite. From the moment she slipped her bony little bottom onto the well-padded dining room chair, she started to eat. "Oh, I think I'll just have the buttered croissants with tea," would be her opening shot, followed in rapid succession by, "and maybe one or two of those little crepes" — and as the waiter was walking away, "and a little Eggs Benedict on the side". Then as we played shuffleboard on the deck and the waiters began to appear for elevenses, Kathy would make a beeline for the nearest deck chair to be ready and waiting as they passed along with tea, coffee and cakes. Kathy was first in the queue for lunch, kept checking her watch as dinnertime approached and tormented the living daylights out of the night stewards for evening snacks. But one night, as we were dressing for dinner, Kathy discovered that she could not fit into her slip. Her skirts and blouses and jeans had all been getting steadily tighter, but she gaily tossed it off with a declaration that all would return to normal once she got her feet back on *terra firma*. However, this bursting slip was disturbing. She'd have to draw a line. No food for Kathy today.

As we settled down to a delicious gourmet breakfast, Gretta glanced up and whispered, "Don't look now, but Kathy's coming in the door in her raincoat." And sure enough, there she was, sashaying across the dining-room floor, head held high with an "I don't know that I'm wearing a raincoat" expression plastered across her smiling face.

Every meal, from then on, followed the same routine. No food for Kathy this morning, or this evening, or tonight — and then the grand entrance, with moonface Kathy waddling across the floor towards our table. And now, even the raincoat was bulging at the seams.

Once we had landed on solid ground, cream cakes became her downfall. The craving started in Bewley's Oriental Cafés on Dublin's Grafton Street, shadowed us into London, and by the time we reached Paris we were dragging her away from one patisserie after another. While the rest of us were in raptures gazing upon the Mona Lisa or strolling along the Champs Elysée, Kathy was furtively combing the backstreets, stalking the patisseries and drooling over cream buns. Betty became her accomplice, but Betty, wrapped in a woollen electric-blue plaid coat that resembled an expensive horse blanket, was hooked on French bread. She never ate it, mind you. She just liked parading around the little squares, French roll tucked under her arm, looking very Parisian and speaking English with a heavy French accent. That no self-respecting French woman would enter a boulangerie and begin a conversation with, "Zis is a mah-vell-uus day, non?" was of no concern to her. She carried on regardless, blithely ignoring disparaging looks and Parisian contempt. She was having a ball!

Strudel became the poison of choice in Germany and by the time we reached Vienna, Kathy had to invest in a new and much larger raincoat. Innsbruck was a real challenge. We hit the town during Wine Festival where the newly plump Kathy held a strong appeal for the older generation of mountain farmers. It must have been her down-home Heidi look, but as polkas played and couples swayed around the floor, Kathy had to be rescued from overly amorous suitors old enough to be her grandfather.

None of us had ever been on skis, so taking to the slopes of the Swiss Alps was not one of our brightest ideas. The money situation was in freefall with Kathy eating her way across the continent and Betty wanting to experience every tourist attraction that came our way. There was certainly nothing left for ski lessons but Betty had taken a shine to the dishy ski instructor and, hell-bent on a mission to impress, we were all taking to the slopes, lessons or no lessons. "For God sake, just how hard can it be?" spat out the bold Betty, as we prevaricated and steered ourselves towards a crackling log fire in the lodge.

"Come on, just look like we know what we're doing. It'll be a blast!" With the imperious Betty taking the lead, we plodded towards the lifts and as the cable car climbed higher and higher over the Alps, defying the natural order of life and swinging in mid-air, Betty swooned with delight while Gretta and I had nervous breakdowns. "Oh, Jesus Christ, what are we doing up here? I hate heights. This is not fun. You've had it, Betty. You're mad! You're not getting another penny from me," moaned a green-faced Gretta who, although the youngest, had been the hard-headed banker on this trip.

"Just how hard can it be?" We positioned ourselves on the top of the green slopes, closed our eyes and pushed off. And down we went, like ten-pins. It took two hours for the rescue team to locate all of us and dig us out. Arms and legs were buried so deep in the snow that we were warned not to attempt to move for fear of breaking our half-frozen limbs. Betty herself was plunged into deep freeze for days after.

Our tour ended in Italy and Italy broke our hearts. I left my heart in Florence, upon the Ponte Vecchio with the River Arno flowing by. Gretta was swept off her feet by the passion and romance of Venice. And Betty and Kathy both capitulated to the magnificence that is Rome.

On the second day of January in the year 1960, I cashed in my return ticket aboard the *SS United States* bound for New York and bought a one-way ticket to Dublin. It had been my goal from the outset. In 1960, the notion of leaving the buzz that was America to strike out on one's own in the backwaters of Ireland would have seemed sheer lunacy. So I needed a plan, and the trip around Europe had given me a plausible exit. Now, following in the footsteps of my father, Michael Joe, I was about to jump ship — but this time, it would be in reverse; from the new world back to the old one.

Gretta, Betty and Kathy continued on to the Canary Islands and then home to New York. As Kathy padded down the ship's gangway, her latest rainwear creation straining across an impressive girth, her parents looked right past her. They didn't know her. When this strange woman threw her arms around them, they were stunned, then horrified. Their precious daughter must have drunk her way across Europe. But two months later, Kathy sent me a picture of her new self, back on home ground, fit and trim once again. Her European flight into gastronomic madness was well and truly behind her.

ࣛ

Ellen Carter and
Michael O'Connell Sr
on their wedding day
in New York city, 1899

Michael Joe O'Connell in 1929, in
the uniform of the 49th Regiment,
"The Fighting Irish" Reserve

Nellie Taaffe in 1928

Nellie Taaffe in 1928

The Taaffe sisters, 1926; rear: Catherine, Mollie; sitting: Nellie, Julia

Nellie and Michael Joe O'Connell, New York, 1932

A recent photograph of No. 488 East 139th Street, The Bronx, home of the O'Connell family

The "South Bronx Five"; (l–r): Eleanor, Gretta, Geraldine, Emmett and Kevin

Most of the O'Connell family in 1946; Michael Joe and Nellie with
(l–r) Eleanor, Gretta, Emmett and Geraldine

Emmett and Geraldine, 1949

Eleanor and Gretta outside No.
445 East 139th Street in 1951

Aunt Della O'Connell Hennigan
with Michael Joe, O'Connell Street,
Dublin, 1955

Aunt Annette O'Connell, 1952

A gathering of the clans: Bronx Gaelic League outing in the Catskill
Mountains, NY, 1958; in the front row, Gretta is seventh from the left,
and Geraldine is twelfth from the left

The Bob Barrett Pipe and Drum Band, 1953; Geraldine is in the back row, first left, while Gretta is in the front, second from left

The Bob Barrett School of Irish Music, 1953; Geraldine is in the front row, first right

On a visit to Sligo, Ireland in 1955; with grandmother Ellen Carter O'Connell (seated) are (l–r): Gretta, Aunt Gretta O'Connell Flynn, Fidelma Flynn and Geraldine

On board the *SS America*, en route to Europe, 1959; (l–r): Shipmate Hans, Gretta, Geraldine, Emmett, Kathy Morgan and Betty Magee

Detective Sergeant Kevin O'Connell of the 41st Precinct, New York City Police Department, 1967

At the christening of Tara Ellen O'Connell, June 1967; Michael Joe is at the rear, fourth from left; Nellie is sitting, third from left; to her left are Geraldine (holding Geraldine Ann), Gretta, Kathy Nolan (holding Tara); front: at left, Kevin Michael, Kevin Sr (holding Sean) and Liam

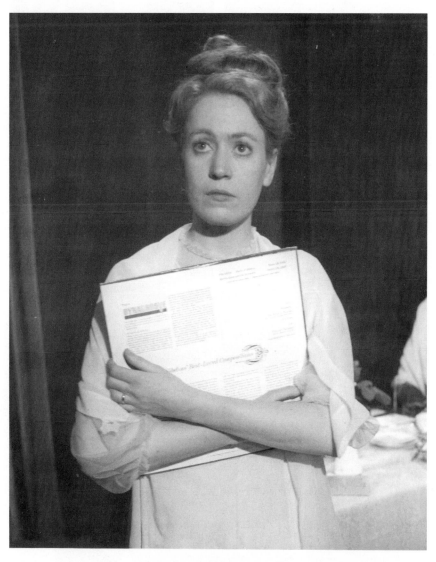

Eleanor O'Connell becomes Eleanora:
on stage at The Actor's Studio, New York, 1963

Eleanor — now Deirdre —
O'Connell, 1964

Luke Kelly, 1964

Luke and Deirdre in 1964

Luke and Deirdre's wedding, 1965, with Maureen and Paddy O'Donoghue

Luke and Deirdre's wedding, with best man Billy Cullen and maid of honour Sabina Coyne (Higgins)

Deirdre, Ciaran Bourke, Luke and Gretta, 1970

Deirdre and Michael Joe in the Garden of Remembrance, Dublin, for the 1966 Easter Rising Commemoration

The Dubliners in Cork with Jack Taaffe (centre); (l–r): John Sheahan, Barney McKenna, Luke, Jim McCann, with Michael O'Keeffe (visiting from Woodside, NY)

The space that was soon to become The Focus Theatre in 1967

Two publicity shots of Deirdre O'Connell in 1978

Deirdre on stage in *La Ronde*
(Arthur Schnitzler) at the
Focus in 1982

Rehearsing at University Hall,
Hatch Street, for *Thérèse Raquin*
(Émile Zola) in 1995

Deirdre outside
Hourican's pub in 1996,
with her ubiquitous
scripts and clipboard

Deirdre outside The Focus Theatre in 1990

Deirdre with three of the
Cusack girls on O'Connell
Street in 1980; (l–r): Breifní,
Geraldine Ann and Aisling

Deirdre near her home at
Dartmouth Square with
Kaniah Ní Chíosóig in 1990

A group of Seminole children from the Ahfachkee School, Big
Cypress Reservation, 1977; Breifní Cusack is in the centre

The Cusacks at the old O'Connell cottage, Ballisodare, Co. Sligo,
2000; (rear, l–r): Kaniah, Aisling, cousin Fidelma Flynn, Geraldine
Ann; (front) Geraldine, holding grandson Connell Ahearne

Chapter 6

RETURN OF THE WILD GEESE

WITH ALL THE ARROGANCE OF YOUTH, I returned to Dublin, certain in the belief that I could make a life in the land that my grandparents and parents had left before me. And once again, my parents, though baffled by the improbability of such a plan, accepted it. If they were shocked or distressed themselves, they never uttered a word of reproach to me. I have no doubt they were relieved that it was to Ireland I had fled, and not some God-forsaken place like Outer Mongolia.

Ireland of the early 1960s was not a world of opportunity. Unemployment was rife and emigration a way of life. And yet, two months after arriving in Dublin, I had landed a job. It had nothing at all to do with my college degree but everything to do with paying the rent. I began work as a Ground Hostess for BKS Air Transport at Dublin Airport for the weekly wage of £13.00 — a very handsome salary at the time. As I saw it, I was the bees' knees.

That was the beginning of reverse emigration in our family, with a steady stream of O'Connells returning to Ireland over the next few years. Emmett and Eleanor were flitting back and forth between the US and Ireland, not yet able to settle fully in either place. And our parents, Nellie and Michael, would come back to Bray, County Wicklow to retire in 1972. The circle that had begun revolving with forced emigrations to America and Australia way back in the 1890s was ever turning.

I had taken a bedsitter on Griffith Avenue, the first of many that saw me traversing the city north and south, from Clare Road to Pleasant Street, back across the Liffey to Clonliffe Road in Drumcondra and then to Marguerite Road in Glasnevin, only to head back south to Harold's Cross. The reason for all the changes? The precarious existence of flat dwellers at the time. There was no permanency of tenure at all. Dublin landlords let rooms out when they needed a few bob and proceeded to throw the tenant out onto the street when that particular need had been met. So for at least three years, I lived out of suitcases, hardly ever unpacking as it just wasn't worthwhile. God only knew when I would receive my next notice to quit.

But I guess I was also somewhat complicit in this itinerant existence because my job sent me all over Britain and I was only too willing to comply. BKS was a British air company engaged in operating a car ferry service between Dublin and Liverpool, as well as passenger services to the North of England and horse transport services to race meetings all over England and the continent. I was "jack of all trades"; sometime reservations agent, sometime grand hostess, and very often aircraft trimmer. And from time to time and whenever the need might arise, I became relief staff for all the other company stations. My favourite station was Nutts Corner Airport in Belfast.

I often wonder at my colossal ignorance at the time. I was young, but youth alone does not fully explain the huge hole that existed in my understanding of life in the North of Ireland. After all, I was reared in a most Irish culture-conscious family, fed on Irish history from birth and I was a Political Science college graduate. I should have had more than a passing knowledge of the divisions and glaring injustices rampant in northern life. But for most people in America, modern Irish history had ended with the Treaty. And as it turned out, I was no more ignorant than the vast majority of my friends who were born and raised in the Republic of Ireland.

Nutts Corner Airport was a big employer in Belfast, with ground staff, maintenance crews, aircraft mechanics and reservations clerks working there for all the main British airlines. And these were top-class jobs. Air hostesses, as flight attendants were then called, were as close to film stars as anyone in Ireland, North or South, was likely to get. Although these much-envied cabin crew were mostly stationed in Britain, ground staff were local and they came a close second in the glamour stakes. The pay was good and the perks fantastic, including low-cost travel to destinations most people could only dream about.

So why were there only four Catholics that I knew about in the total airport workforce? These were the Kelly sisters, Marie and Eileen, from the Whiterock Road, West Belfast, Eileen Donnelly from Ballycastle, County Antrim and myself, a Dublin hiree. And we all worked for BKS.

The *craic* at the airport was mighty and everyone got along famously. Nobody ever mentioned religion. But the *craic* never extended beyond the airport. They went to their dances and we went to ours and never the twain did meet.

It was normal company policy to provide a special transport bus to pick the staff up at different points in the city because very few people owned private cars. My pick-up point was in front of a graffiti-sprayed wall on the Shankill Road which invited all and sundry to "Kick the Pope". The bus didn't go into Catholic areas and it didn't occur to me to complain. That was just the way things were.

Was this the same person who, at seventeen years of age, had transferred colleges in New York because the Reverend Mother wanted to change her accent? The same person who decided to see the world and did? The same person who took off for Europe on a visit and stayed for a lifetime?

It was. But the political and cultural climate in Belfast was oh, so different. Let no one say that cultural climate is unimportant or not a determining factor in social behaviour. In New York, I had a certain crisis of identity, not knowing whether I was Irish or American, but I never had a crisis when it came to knowing my rights. I was as good as anyone else. I was just as smart and just as entitled. And I was brought up in a society that told me to exercise those rights. Had I been born black in Alabama, it might have been a very different story. I might have understood a lot better what was going on in the North.

Belfast in the 1960s was stuck in the eighteenth century. I was a Catholic and I was an anomaly. I had a job and, man, was I ever thankful to have such a good job. I couldn't afford to lose my job. Crossing the road to get the bus was just the way things were.

On an individual level, within the comfort of the workplace, Protestants and Catholics got along. But Catholics never ventured into the crowds because crowds could easily become mobs and mobs have no conscience. Today, I cringe to think of it. At the time, I knew no better.

CB

BUOYED BY MY SPECTACULAR SUCCESS in the Irish jobs market, my brother Emmett decided to settle in Dublin a year later. He was staying in Dublin's Summerhill with two IRA veterans, Dick and Maude Mulready. Dick had been interned in the Curragh during World War II and Maude was imprisoned following the ill-fated IRA campaign in England in the early 1940s. As a result, Maude's health wasn't the best. Emmett had been working as a draughtsman in Dublin for over a year, with a firm of consultant engineers, when Dick offered to sell him his house. He was retiring from work and wanted to move to Bray to take advantage of the sea air. Never one to miss an opportunity, Emmett bought it and shortly thereafter, I moved my well-worn suitcases into my brother's first house on North Summer Street.

I had been back in Dublin for just a short spell, and still working at the airport, when I spotted an intriguing advertisement in the *Sunday Times* for an excursion to Russia. It was an all-inclusive tour, setting out on a Russian liner from Tilbury Landing in the South of England with a contingent of British Socialists and from there it was sailing on to Le Havre to pick up a complement of French Communists. It would then proceed along the North Sea with stops at Copenhagen and Stockholm, into the Baltic Sea, through the Kiev Canal and docking finally at Leningrad for the 44th Anniversary of the Storming of the Winter Palace. The final leg of the journey would be by rail to Moscow for the annual November celebrations of the 1917 Revolution. This was most definitely for me.

But why was a twenty-two-year-old Irish-American girl, who had taken up residence in Ireland, attracted to such a quixotic journey in the first place?

It was because childhood memories filled my head; memories of furious arguments around the kitchen table, and on the sidewalk outside St Jerome's Church, and on the front stoops of our houses in the Bronx — memories of bitter disputes about Russia and Communism, America and Capitalism, Ireland and Catholicism and Republicanism. These lofty themes had been the common currency of my childhood and childhood memories are not soon forgotten.

I had gone on to read a lot and study some but I had not yet managed to untangle much. I had lived in the North. I had seen the injustices. The Civil Rights Movement was stirring in America. It was time to figure things out for myself — to discover the measure of truth or lies in that explosive childhood mix.

When Emmett got wind of my imminent departure for the Soviet Union, he became apoplectic. Notwithstanding the fact that he had recently married his girlfriend of six weeks, Ray O'Kelly from Dublin, he was determined that the *M.V. Mikhail Kalinin* would not leave England without him. Ray must have been an extraordinary woman because, although she had no intention of travelling herself, she threw herself headlong into the rush to get Emmett a visa to enter the USSR.

All my travel arrangements were signed and sealed and in proper order. After all, I hadn't just come back from a honeymoon! So off I flew to London to stay with colleagues from work and to wait for Emmett's imminent arrival with his passport and special entry visa.

But Emmett was back in Dublin spinning in circles, running from the American Embassy to the Irish passport office, then back to the American Embassy and finally on to the General Post Office in order to contact the Russian consulate in London. This was 1962 during the peak of the Cold War, the era of Sputniks, Cuban missiles, hydrogen bombs and missile defence. It was the age of the arctic freeze between East and West, between Nikita Khrushchev and John Fitzgerald Kennedy. It was also the era of two-year waiting lists for telephone lines in Dublin City. Only the fortunate few private Irish citizens had telephone lines. Everyone else queued at the GPO.

Reconnaissance day in London came and went with no sign of Emmett. So I trundled off to Tilbury Landing alone, only to be met by the bold Emmett who had arrived just minutes before me, with a valid visa — but without a valid passport.

CB

"MERCIFUL GOD. Have you lost your reason?" I exploded. "You think you can head off to Russia without a passport? And you expect to get back alive? Are you completely mad?"

"Calm down. It's not as bad as you think," muttered Emmett in a conspiratorial whisper, so as not to draw undo attention to himself among this confederation of Socialists, Communists and just plain, good old-fashioned militants. "I've been given a visa, right? My passport was out of date, and I had to get a new one, which I did, but in all the kerfuffle, I left it on the dresser. I've rung Ray and she'll post it to me in care of the ship. When it gets here, they can send it on to the ship in Le Havre and I can collect it there."

That's when I completely lost the head. "You really are out of your mind, aren't you? Have you cleared this with the Russians? No, I didn't think so. But you think that this ship's commander, or captain, or whatever he is, is going to take you on board without a valid passport because you've had a little problem with the post?"

"Hang on," Emmett continued to whisper in a disgustingly rational tone, "We'll just wait until everyone else is on board and then we'll explain the situation to the captain."

"Oh, right. That's a great idea. But just when did this performance become '*we*'? I have my passport! Remember?"

"Correct," continued Emmett, all reason and good sense. "And all the more reason for him to believe us."

I could not believe what I was hearing. We were in the middle of the Cold War, for the love of God! But according to Emmett, this captain, whom we hadn't even set eyes on yet, was going to take him under his wing with love and concern and something like, "Your passport's going to be a luttle late? Wull, dun't worry, my son, we wull take care of everything."

Emmett laughed but started to go a pale shade of grey as the queue got shorter and shorter and we got nearer and nearer to passport control. The plan was that I would go through first, all proper and correct, and then I would present my brother, the madman with the little problem.

Up I went to the passport officials, brimming with goodness and light, smiling and scraping. And, oh Jesus. Did that hurt. But I could have saved myself the searing shame. They looked at me like *I* was mad. So I rushed on to introduce my brother. "Now smart ass," I thought, "you're on your own."

Emmett was the very soul of propriety. "Gentlemen," he began, "I have a little problem. You see, my passport's on its way here from Dublin. It was meant to be here before departure but since it looks like we're about ready to sail, I don't think it's going to catch me on time. So I was thinking that, maybe, the Captain could take me on board and I'm sure it'll get to Le Havre before we do." How he figured that out, I have no idea. But on he went. "And if it doesn't, well I'll just eject myself from the tour. I know what a difficult decision this will be and I certainly don't want to add to the Captain's discomfort in any way."

"Whose discomfort?" I nearly screeched! "Well of all the unmitigated gall!" But Emmett just stood there, beseeching eyes turned on uncomprehending officialdom. The faces in front of us were stoic, their beady little eyes betraying nothing. "Christ Almighty," I thought, squirming in the spotlight with this madman of a brother. "How can you win a war against the likes of this? Every single thought is written across my face. Theirs are blank sheets."

"Have you any other personal identification," asked one of the stone-faced Soviets. "Yes," replied my charming brother, now only too happy to be of assistance. "I have my Irish gun licence." Oh, Jesus, Mary and Joseph, help us!

Off they went to fetch the captain and, momentarily, a scowling lump of a man stood in front of us. Honest to God, I felt like we were heading for the gallows. But no, truth being stranger than fiction, this forbidding looking captain of the *M.V. Kalinin* agreed to take Emmett on board, under his personal protection and without the essential documentation. The only proviso was that he couldn't leave the ship until the papers arrived. We were flabbergasted. Just imagine some unfortunate Russian trying to spin a yarn like that in America, with its national neurosis of suspecting Commies under every bed. It just wouldn't happen. But here we were, sailing off to the USSR in the middle of the Cold War, with Russia threatening to blow the US off the face of the earth and vice versa, under the care of a Russian ship's captain.

Predictably, there was no sign of the wayward passport when we reached Le Havre, yet Emmett was not offloaded. It would definitely catch up with us at the next port of call, Copenhagen, where we were to have a day ashore. "Some people are just born under a lucky star," thought I.

When it didn't, Emmett was shattered, consigned as he was to his stuffy little cabin while the rest of us sauntered off in search of the Tivoli Gardens with the dinky little mermaid perched up on a rock. This trailing passport was becoming a shared shipboard concern. If it did not turn up in Stockholm, Emmett would see Russia from his port hole. It seemed like his lucky star was beginning slowly to tarnish.

Well, now, who exactly was on board this floating university of the Revolution? Jerome, who was an American Baptist from Louisiana, a Welshman named Martin Thomas, an Australian girl about my own age, and ourselves. The remainder of the 350 passengers were all raging Communists.

There was no shuffleboard, no swimming pool and no ballroom on this ship. The main features were the library and the bar. The library was stacked from floor to ceiling with the latest copies of revolutionary gazettes from around the world. Then there were the writings of Karl Marx and Vladimir Lenin in twenty-seven different languages, including Esperanto. This was the new language of the world, very love-and-flowers sixties and specifically constructed so that regardless of one's native tongue, this language would provide a common link. There was even a tutor on board who conducted classes in Esperanto for three hours every day, so that those of us who didn't speak Russian could converse with ordinary people on our arrival. I guess the organisers assumed we were all good Communists and would not be into spreading any offensive western propaganda to the natives.

Jerome, Martin, Julianne, Emmett and I were disgracefully negligent, giving Esperanto a wide berth and spending most of our time chatting with the crew in the comfort of the bar. I had been doing Russian in night classes at UCD over the previous year and had also been taking extra lessons with a Russian émigré whose husband had been a soldier in the Tsar's army. They had fled the turmoil of the 1917 Revolution and had arrived in England to make a new life. But World War II, with all of its convolutions, had intervened and a handful of them departed for the safety of neutral Ireland. A big, old rambling house in Ranelagh, Dublin became their home.

I was doing famously with this wobbly tongue until Madame Lipskaya decided that I had to learn to write properly in Russian script. With dim lighting, damp paper and a balalaika plucking away in a distant room, I fell into a nightly trance, tracing the curling letters and implanting fascinating little accents here and there on the page. I was becoming a very respectable calligrapher, but my linguistic fluency was slowing down dramatically. Nonetheless, I could make myself understood and that would have to do.

Apart from a gut-wrenching 1,000-proof Russian vodka, beer and Cherry Heering were the only other available drinks on board. There were a few other peculiarities as well. The bread that was not consumed at breakfast reappeared for lunch and if it wasn't demolished at that sitting, well it just came back again for dinner. We quickly learned to eat everything the first time. A watery red cabbage soup called *borsht* also came to the table three times a day, mostly accompanied by some indeterminate type of fish, and only once by meat. That was a red-letter day, the occasion of the Captain's Dinner.

But God forgive my uneducated palate, for if I had had the fortitude to persevere at Marymount, I would have revelled in the red and black caviar that sat in the middle of the table beside the salt, pepper and margarine; simply lashings of it. This was, after all, an educational experience, I told myself. So I should learn to like it. No different from learning Russian. I forced myself, meal after meal, to indulge, gagging with every mouthful of the foul stuff, its gelatine-like eyes shimmering away malevolently at me from the middle of the table.

Bread wasn't the only substance to return with unexpected regularity. I couldn't get rid of my snagged and torn nylon tights either. No matter how often I put them into the bin in my cabin, the room stewardess would retrieve them and place them carefully across my bed. It was, undoubtedly, inconceivable to her that anyone would knowingly throw away something as valuable as that. Or was honesty an inbred virtue of the USSR?

After Copenhagen, we steamed along into the Kiev Canal and exited it with Poland to the south and Sweden to the north, and only then did the nerve ends begin to fray. By now, most of the ship was in on the Captain's dilemma. He had undertaken to trust Emmett, believing that the necessary visa to enter the USSR would arrive before disembarkation. But it wasn't in Stockholm and, once again, Emmett was bound into custody. Jerome, a very dubious brand of Baptist who swilled vodka and beer with abandon, had become fast friends with Emmett, and Julianne and I were equally good mates. So, we felt like a band of traitors as we set off to wander the city's winding streets and majestic squares, to sample Swedish breads and Swedish beers, while Emmett was left standing forlornly on the ship's deck.

Our only hope now was that the visa had been sent directly on to Leningrad, bypassing all other stops along the way. We headed into the Gulf of Finland, passing the medieval city of Tallinn, then steamed on past Helsinki and suddenly the glittering splendour of Leningrad came into view. Our miserable hopes were quickly dashed. There was no sign of the elusive passport.

Captain Semeonov called Emmett to his cabin and we were all prepared for the worst. Jerome, Julianne and I had been directed to a room on the dock that served as the immigration centre as well as the bank. After clearing immigration, we went on to change dollars into roubles and we were firmly instructed to spend it all. There would be no exchange of roubles back into dollars and we, most definitely, would not be allowed to take roubles out of the country. "As if . . ." we thought, as we glumly waited for Emmett's sentence to be passed.

The rest of our contingent was briskly moving towards the waiting train and we were sternly advised to do likewise. Emmett would have to look after himself. But as we approached our designated carriage, a military jeep careered into sight and in the rear seat sat Emmett, waving mightily with a broad grin spread across his face.

"Right, comrades, we're on our way. I'm free! No visa and no passport — the immigration people are holding onto my visa — but now I've got a letter on the off-chance that I'm stopped for ID. It's written in Russian with a telephone contact number. Who would believe it?" We quickly piled into the train to Moscow, just in case there was a sudden change of heart.

೮ಽ

WHEN ONE LOOKS AT AN ATLAS of the former USSR and Asia and considers the vastness of empty space stretching across Eurasia, Russia appears to be smack in the middle of Europe. Leningrad, with her endless banks of gilded colonnades, her gracious river walks and imposing cathedrals is truly the Paris of the East. But Moscow, 200 kilometres inland, is another story altogether.

We were comfortably sheltered in compact little sleeper compartments as our train rattled out of the city station. Within less than half an hour we were in a foreign land. The friendly comfort of familiar shapes and the soft pools of lamplight on Leningrad's cobbled streets were all gone. I scraped aside the frost that had settled on the glass panes of the train's corridors and studied the rustic scenes rumbling by.

It was a litany of one despondent and wind-blown shanty town after another. Limp little wisps of smoke rose from lonesome wooden shacks. Bare tree limbs strained under the weight of snow and ice. Frozen lakes shimmered in the moonlight. Night had settled in this, the frozen north, and the conductor advised us to retire to our bunks. We would reach Moscow just before dawn.

It was the second of November and we arrived in the middle of a snow storm; not that there is anything odd about snow storms in Moscow, but it did send shivers up and down my spine. Doughty great figures wrapped in voluminous dark garments, topped with black fur hats and wearing mittens that looked like bears' claws, scurried through the white blizzard. A knifing cold wind cut through my heavy winter coat. I would need to get weatherproofed fast.

"Pinch me," yelped Julianne as we unpacked our bags and filled the chunky old dressers with our belongings. "This is the classiest place in town. There's the Moscow River right outside our door. My ma's never going to believe this." All of the tour's guests were being accommodated in various hostelries around the city and we had hit pay dirt. All four of us were in the Hotel Europa.

An official guide from the state *Intourist* Office summoned all the guests to an orientation briefing in the hotel's ballroom, just minutes after our arrival. They weren't wasting any time! These visitors were on a sacred pilgrimage. This was no different from a Muslim visiting Mecca or a Catholic visiting the Vatican.

A very stylishly dressed young woman with the voice and carriage of a matron addressed us in sombre tones. "You are all very wulcome to Rossia," she began in lightly accented English, scanning the gathering and resting her eyes on four obvious interlopers lurking around the fringes. "Now, there are some things you most understand. You have an official guide — me. I yam entrosted to take you to see the places of in-ter-est in Moscow. What you want to see, you tull me. I wull take you there and I wull tull you everything you want to know. Bot, I think, perhaps, some one of you would like to see Moscow alone?" looking straight at us, "and so, I wull tell you this. You can do that, bot you must tell me where you wull be. We do not want to loo-s anyone." Message clearly delivered and message well received. We couldn't ask for fairer than that.

Jerome and Emmett took off in one direction and Julianne and I in another, but all heading towards Gorky Street. We had arranged to meet up again in the dining room for dinner that evening.

೦ಜ

WESTERN VISITORS TO RUSSIA were not exactly ten-a-penny in 1962. The Iron Curtain was drawn tight and the Central Committee of the Communist Party held a firm grip on power. The US and the USSR were locked in a dangerous arms race and all patriotic Russian eyes were fastened on space. The "Sputnik" had given America a black eye and President Kennedy had vowed to avenge American honour. This old world was becoming a very jumpy place in which to be.

At the same time, but in marked contrast to the nervous world of the CIA, MI5 and the KGB, a new generation of love freaks was raising its dazzling head. The hippies, all frizzy hair, love-beads and flowers and wrapped up in a dizzying psychedelic package, were blossoming in the West. "Tune in, turn on and drop out" was their mantra, with Dr Timothy Leary and Allen Ginsberg the high priests of love fests. Russian youths of that same generation were making their own clandestine forays into public parks with illicit transistor radios and tuning into Radio Free Europe after dark.

"You speak English?" A whisper through immobile lips. "Please, not to turn. Please, to sit on bench."

"What the blazes was that?"

Two well-dressed young men were tripping on our heels, as Julianne and I marvelled at empty windows in empty department stores. They said no more and my legs began to buckle as I stole a quick glance. They looked normal enough from what I could see; no short thick necks, no thick squat bodies, no red puffed-up faces, no evil-slitted eyes. But feeling under severe pressure to obey, we did what we were told and sat down on the bench in front of us.

"Please to look straight ahead. Not to look at us."

"Oh, Sweet Jesus, what is going on? What did we do now?" My heart was racing and my temples pounding.

"Look," I said, not daring to turn my head, "I have my passport and my visa and I'm just a tourist and we're just sightseeing and . . ." I was stopped short.

"I am Villy — my friend is Viktor. We are students. We talk to you."

"Oh, thank you, Lord." My heart stopped racing and my temples quit throbbing. I started to breathe again.

"We are artists. We are puppeteers. We are Moscow Puppet Theatre. Please, you can meet tonight after theatre? I wull wear my western coat. You wull see me."

Come again? Wear his western coat? "Sorry?" I said, still looking straight ahead and talking into thin air. "I don't know what you mean. What's a western coat?"

"I have coat from the west. I wull wear this. Then I can talk to you. Secret Police wull not see me."

"Secret Police?" I nearly screamed. "You don't mean to say they're watching us!"

"Maybe so. Maybe no. But we wull meet and we wull talk."

They got up and left and we watched their backs disappearing into the crowd. We'd never recognise them again. We still hadn't seen their faces. The second one never spoke. What the hell had just happened?

We continued our walk along Gorky Street but now, seeing nothing and everything at once, still trying to figure out if we had been hallucinating. My eyes were darting everywhere. What do the Secret Police look like? Could that be one, that wizened old man squatting against a door and staring at everyone who passed by? Or that plump and motherly looking woman brushing up against me with her plastic shopping basket? Or that newsman on the corner? Or all three?

"We'd better go back to the hotel and figure out what we're going to do. See if the boys ran into any strange women propositioning them on Gorky Street," I said.

As it turned out, they hadn't met any artists or actors or the like but had run into plenty of immobile lips trying to buy the clothes off their backs. You could raise a fortune overnight in black market Levis. But what could you do with the roubles?

Nothing to buy, can't take them out of the country and can't change them back into dollars. And life in the Archipelago wasn't a very tempting notion.

Stop the music! What astounding good luck! Madame Patlova was planning to take the group to the Puppet Theatre that night. Perfect! We would love to join them.

It was hard to concentrate on the humanlike puppets, fascinating and all as they were. Julianne and I were craning our necks in the hopes of catching a glimpse of these artists. But no such luck. Just horrid little faces painted up like witches and goblins, jumping up and down and doing mad things in Russian. Kind of like you would see in Haight Ashbury in San Francisco, minus the weed.

At the end of the performance, we dawdled in the lobby, thoroughly engrossed in puppeteering history, closely scrutinising every photograph and every showcase until the last person had gone. Then we slipped out front and waited. For what or for whom? A western coat?

Out of the shadows stepped the two artists. Sort of like that movie, *The Third Man*. Viktor and Villy. And he in the coat!

And then came the explanation. Villy's father was a diplomat serving at the United Nations building in New York and in such an exalted state he had access to certain luxury items, like Jack Daniels and Abercrombie and Fitch. Villy wore his western tweed whenever he wanted to throw the secret hounds off his scent. He would not attract unwelcome attention in his western gear, not the way a typical Russian would. Fraternisation with the enemy was not encouraged. To the Secret Police, he looked like a tourist.

"Well now," I thought to myself, "It takes more than a coat to turn a Russian into an American" — which is what Villy was pretending to be. But what the heck! Why burst his bubble? As long as we were safe.

So, we walked and we talked and we walked some more. Villy and Viktor and Julianne and I. They invited us into a bar for a drink. Great! Except we weren't allowed to talk. And we all had to stand. There were no chairs or seats or stools at all in this bar. And the place was lit up like a carnival. You walked up to a tureen that looked like our canteen coffee machines, placed your glass under it, and out came pure vodka. Down the hatch, and leave; that was the drill. Congregating to discuss the issues of the day was clearly something else not to be encouraged.

Viktor was a student of music at the Conservatory in Leningrad and was only working in the theatre part-time. Villy didn't seem to need to work; in fact, he seemed pretty well-off. So what about this classless society? Surely all Russians didn't enjoy a standard of living like this?

It seems some were more equal than others. Everybody had a job. The streets were spotless with women in babushkas sweeping and sweeping, endlessly sweeping. The underground ran on the honour system. No inspectors, no ticket collectors, no fuss, no dirt, and priceless works of art adorning marble train platforms unmolested. But I had eyes to see and I had seen the shanty towns.

Then I had to remind myself that we had that particular social calamity in America and England and Ireland too. Plus, we had rampant unemployment. So who was I to throw bricks?

And then we came to the serious stuff. The "you must understand me" kind of stuff.

Viktor had been very quiet through all of this. Villy was the worldly wise, the cosmopolitan Russian. But Viktor was passionately Russian. "We are Russian and we are proud to be Russian. But we want to go outside Russia. Every year, every Russian go to Black Sea for rest. This is good, no? This is good. But I have not passport. I cannot go outside Russia. I want to see how you live. I want to see all things. But I am Russian, so I cannot."

There was a serious tug-of-war going on here, pride and loyalty to country against a hunger for knowledge of the outside world. They held a deep loyalty to the system that had put bread on their tables, sputniks into space, and young musicians like themselves into conservatories. At the same time, they really did go into parks in the dead of night and listen to scrambled American radio. They wanted photos of our houses, and our families, and our houses, and our friends, and our houses. I was getting a little paranoid with all this talk about our houses until Villy offered to show me his.

"You wull come to my house tomorrow. We wull meet here, by Moskva River. Then we wull walk. It wull be OK!" He loved that expression. Everything would be OK!

"I wull take you where you want to go. To shop, to bar, to anywhere. You don't talk. It wull be OK!" It was heartbreaking, really, this desperate need to present everything in Russia as OK.

We returned late to the hotel and the boys turned back before we got there, still walking in the safety of the shadows. A wild jazz session was going on in the ballroom with Aker Bilk's "Midnight in Moscow" stirring the night. And now it was Emmett's turn for a mad story.

A clutch of Czech businessmen had been drinking all night at the table next to himself and Jerome and the more lubricated their tonsils became, the chattier they became. "American, yes? Irish? You Catholic? Me Catholic. Look." And out of his pocket, he pulled a pair of rosary beads. This was in 1962, in the centre of atheistic, communistic Russia!

ﻌ

THE NEXT DAY, I was at the appointed spot at the appointed time and Villy arrived. We set off in the direction of his house, and on the way, I discovered that he had been married but was now divorced. He was all of 22! This was different!

But it got better and now I really was impressed. He was the grandson, or godson, or some such relation to the great Boris Pasternak and therefore his family got to live in an apartment house reserved for writers and their families. This was the system in Russia. You may not make a whole heap of money, but you got perks, and a good apartment amounted to a serious one. The way I see things going in this crazy money-driven world, it doesn't seem like a bad one either.

We took the lift upstairs and entered the apartment. Villy had already told me that he lived with his parents, but I have no idea what the apartment looked like or how big it was or who was in it because we walked from the hall door straight into Villy's bedroom. What the hell!

It was small. A bed, a table and a chair. I sat on the chair. There was a knock on the door, Villy opened it slightly and a hand appeared in the cracked doorway, holding a plate of chocolates. The hand withdrew and the door closed. Who was that? No idea. No explanation and no questions asked. Then Villy rooted under his bed and came up with a stack of magazines. He could have knocked me over with a feather. "Amerika" is what they were called and on the cover of the latest edition was that famous picture of John F. Kennedy's handsome face looking full into the camera with Jackie in serene profile. This was the twilight zone! Then came another knock on the door, the same hand appeared with another plate — this time the plate was piled with biscuits.

This two-step reached comical proportions over the next hour as the distended hand appeared and withdrew at regular intervals while I sat gaping at very slick and very appealing American propaganda. Villy was an unabashed Yankee lover. He beat out *Tuxedo Junction* on his desktop, doo-dahding away in a reverie of bliss. It began to dawn on me that Villy had a comfortable cushion behind him; he was so well connected that he could afford to be brash. Others might not be this daring.

Our East-meets-West interlude was quickly gaining momentum and the next rendezvous was arranged for Viktor's apartment with a collection of his friends from the Music Conservatory in Leningrad. "It's like a police line-up," I thought as I sat in the middle of this group of staring Russians. They looked me over carefully, from head to toe, taking in every detail of my appearance, unashamedly fingering the material in my corduroy mini-skirt and tracing the patterns of my fair-isle woollen jumper. Satis-fied that the physical inspection was totally complete, they moved on to the interview, covering everything from my family to my studies and on to my hopes for the future. "I am like a Martian among earthlings," I thought, trying desperately to hold on to a few last shreds of dignity.

Then Viktor, our host, placed a small glass tumbler in front of each of us and several bottles of vodka in the middle of a nearby table. Our glasses were partially filled and one by one the guests began to raise their toasts.

"To friendship!" Everybody was grinning, glasses were clink-ing and down the hatch went neat one hundred per cent proof vodka. "To music and art!" as smiles got broader and glasses fuller. "To Russia!" with voices rising and chests swelling. "To the United States of America!" and hysterical giggling all round. "To Nikita Khrushchev!" rapidly followed by "John F. Kennedy!" and by this time all formalities had fallen away. We were now into the realm of address exchanges and passionate promises to write. "But won't our letters be censored?" I asked, so pumped full of western propaganda was I. "Maybe they will and maybe they won't. But we will write anyway." Once again, there it was, that determined doggedness in the face of such a mighty political ma-chine. It made me feel very small.

 CB

ON THE 7TH OF NOVEMBER, a colossal show of strength marched past the chilling presence of Comrade Vladimir Lenin in Red Square. "What terrible secrets are sealed inside that tomb of concrete and steel?" I wondered. Shafts of winter sunlight streamed down on an austere podium lined with the truculent faces of Russian force, their stocky, forbidding figures enveloped incongruously in fluffy fur collars and coats. Nikita Khrushchev and Leonid Brezhnev were centre-stage.

The full might of the USSR was on display for all the world to see; thousands and thousands of spine-tingling, goose-stepping feet, eyes and arms raised in solemn salute as they stormed past Lenin's grim and brooding mausoleum, wave after wave of blood-red flags emblazoned with the hammer and sickle of a defiant proletariat, armies of loyal factory workers and platoons of plodding peasant farmers. Finally, battalions of army tanks rumbled past and the millions trembled. We were gazing on the pride of Russian science and genius, the miracle that had catapulted Russia ahead of the Americans, the secret weapon that had shot them into the Space Age: the Sputnik.

In 1962, Russia was the master of the universe, holding the world in the grip of fear. But as Emmett, Jerome, Julianne and I boarded the train for Leningrad, our Russian friends, once strangers painted as enemies, gathered on the platform, waving and weeping and blowing kisses. We all knew that the tentative parting of the Iron Curtain that had transpired over the past few short days would more than likely be firmly and finally slammed shut.

To my utter amazement, one of my letters did get through and here was the reply. It was written in Russian, but Villy included his own English translation.

> *C.C.C.P. Mockva*
> *NabpyuuHckuu nep.*
> *g. No. 17, nb. No. 45*
> *Juagkoby B.5.*
> *11 December 1962*

Dear Geraldine,

A merry Christmas!

Besides that, I wish you a happy New Year. 31ˢᵗ December at 12 o'clock by New York time I shall drink your health, happiness and success. Viktor and Sasha also wish you many happy days.

I remember these times in Mockva very often and my heart fills with sorrow as you are very far now. Thank you, that you remember us. I was very glad to receive your letter, but I read it with great difficulty, even through the magnifying glass, as your handwriting is not clear.

As before, I live well. Now I don't work, and only study. The work took from me plenty of time. I want to go to Leningrad during winter vacation. Now the weather is none too cold in Moscow.

I am very sorry I had no time to present something you with for memory, but I think I shall do it in future. I hope you will be able to write to me some more and we will receive your letters.

Hearty congratulations to your family and friends in the West.

All the most best, your friend,

Villy

But there was no future. That was the last I ever heard. I have often wondered, since the fall of Communism in the East, what the lives of Villy and Viktor and Sasha are like in the convulsion that is Russia of today. No doubt, with their new-found freedoms, they will have finally breached those once impregnable walls. As the clash of cultures become muted and former desires become needs, as Coca Cola and McDonalds invade Moscow and the Russian mafia invade the Cote D'Azur, I wonder now if the cold, harsh winds of capitalism have blurred their youthful dreams.

CB

Chapter 7

ACTORS PREPARE

B UT TIDE AND TIME WAIT FOR NO MAN, and swirling around in the mediocrity of Parkchester, New York, was an evolving and radically changing Eleanor O'Connell. She was now immersed in the chaotic world of young hopefuls and Parkchester was nowhere anyone with visions wanted to be. The time had come to leave the home that Kevin, Emmett and I had already departed. Eleanor moved to the centre of her universe, to lower Manhattan, to share apartments and dreams with a close circle of friends who would remain loyal companions through all the turmoil that would mark her later life. Paula Vanesse, Michael Graine — and Barbara Streisand, that bold and brash young singer from Brooklyn with a voice that would become the hallmark of the decade. As Barbara's name became the more enigmatic Barbra, Eleanor's became Eleanora. Her acting career was in the ascendant.

Eleanora had won a scholarship to the Dramatic Workshop at the New School for Social Research and was working a six-day week, engaged in everything from sewing curtains to painting and building sets, and for seven hours daily she was immersed in the Stanislavsky programme. In an interview for "Dublin Women in the Arts" in 1980, Eleanora explained what the programme meant to her:

> "It was Stanislavsky who really built my personality. The programme, and I prefer to call it a programme rather than a method, emphasises internal technique, which was the very

reason I went into acting in the first place. During the first year, we never touched a script. The things we worked on, the cornerstones of the programme, were relaxation, imagination, and emotional development; intense knowledge and use of oneself serve as the basis for any characterisation.

"It can be a painful process, but it builds up the strengths you feel you have, pins down those things you identify with and enables you to sense and objectify them. You come out of it much more aware, a deeper and broader human being."

Eleanora's visits "home" to Ireland became more frequent, however brief. Acting is "all pain, all guts, all inside", she would explain, balling her fists and beating her breasts and leaving Emmett and me mesmerised with the agony of it all. No longer the charming ingénue, Eleanora was undergoing a metamorphosis of body and soul. She was acting and teaching at the Dramatic Workshop's Repertory Theatre and appearing in all the great twentieth-century classics so revered by its founder, the gifted Erwin Piscator.

It was after one of these small off-Broadway productions that she was spotted by Lee Strasberg and invited to join the Actor's Studio. This was home for all the main proponents of the Stanislavsky system in American theatre. Icons of American stage and screen such as Montgomery Clift, James Dean and Marlon Brando had studied there in the 1950s. Ten years later, Eleanora was invited to join that illustrious roll call.

Constantin Stanislavsky, the Russian actor, director, producer and teacher, was born in Moscow in 1863 and died in 1939. During his life, he made two significant contributions to world theatre. He founded the Moscow Art Theatre with Nemirovich-Danchenko and built that theatre into one of the most famous acting units the world has ever known. Fundamental to his belief system was the principle that theatre, and in particular the Moscow Art Theatre, must be a teacher of man and society.

Secondly, he formulated the Stanislavsky system of acting based on the works of Tolstoy, Gorky and Chekhov, who were his great friends. The truths found in the works of this triumvirate are based on the belief that every man must bring out the best within him and that every man has a deep longing to do so. "These great writers preached the dignity of man and man's eternal quest to find himself and his purpose in life. They encouraged the freedom of all men and women's yearning to liberate all that is good within him." This is taken from the *Complete Works of Stanislavsky* presented by the Stanislavsky Institute in London and it is the philosophy that ordered Deirdre's future life.

The root of the Stanislavsky system is the belief that in order for a person to become a great actor, he must first become a better human being. As this person improves in his personal being, he is then able to release a superior power, which becomes visible to everyone, and which is called great acting. Over many, many years, Stanislavsky perfected a series of principles for the development of these qualities in the artist. He lived by these principles and spent the rest of his life trying to persuade anyone who came within his circle to believe in them. Finally, his genius overcame tremendous opposition to his radical new ideas, and the Stanislavsky system went on to inform every facet of Russian artistic life.

Ultimately, Stanislavsky believed that the system was critical to good theatre and he devoted the greatest part of his life to teaching it. Teaching the system was his passion. In this, Eleanora became his true disciple.

Eleanora had much earlier made up her mind that she would find fulfilment only in Ireland. The dream of returning to Dublin, to set up her own drama school in tandem with the finest repertory theatre in the land, stayed with her while she worked in New York, performing Arthur Miller, Tennessee Williams and Eugene O'Neill, Chekhov and Strindberg, Ibsen, Sartre and Beckett.

To build her growing theatre fund, Eleanora continued to sing in coffee houses and cafés around Greenwich Village, embracing the protest culture of Joan Baez and Bob Dylan and sharing a stage with them at the Newport Folk Festival. But singing was only a means to an end — never the end in itself. In 1961, Eleanora dropped her given name, adopting instead all the power and passion of the mythical Deirdre, and with her big dreams and small treasures, Deirdre O'Connell headed off for Dublin.

Her New York colleagues were stunned. She was well on the road to a glittering career, one that would be paved with fame and fortune. She was surrendering all of that to embark on a foolish dream, what they referred to as her "Celtic twilight". What hidden forces drew this rising young actor away from the epicentre of American theatre to a comparative backwater on the edge of Europe?

Eleanor had grown up in a culture that straddled two worlds, a culture in which Ireland and America were inextricably linked. The transition from one to the other was not difficult, at first, because the lines were so badly blurred. However, as she grew older, that transition became more fraught. Life choices had to be made.

Had Eleanor been born of small farming stock in Currarague, County Cork in the year 1939, the odds of her reaching success in her life's chosen path would have been stacked against her. Furthermore, the chances of rising to prominence in her art at such a young age would have been slim to nil. Social exclusion would have seen to that.

Instead, she had been born in the Bronx and blessed at birth with beauty, brains and talent. Throughout her childhood, her parents had given her great measures of courage and self-belief. America gave her opportunity.

Like the rest of the South Bronx Five, Eleanor struggled with divided loyalties.

Some emigrants can leave their homeland behind, adopt a new culture, make a new life and never look back. Others carry the homeland with them, forever haunted by visions of what should have been — but could not be. It might be Ireland, Germany, Poland, Russia or Pakistan. The homelands are vastly different, but the longing is the same.

It is the curse of emigration; that inexplicable spiritual tug, the umbilical cord that ties. For emigrants such as these, the cord is never successfully severed. They carry it with them for life and they pass it on to their descendants. It becomes a troubling inheritance.

That inexplicable tug brought Eleanor back to Ireland and kept her in Ireland for the rest of her life. She consigned the young and dreamy Eleanor, Ellie and Eleanora to America. She became the formidable Deirdre O'Connell of Dublin Focus Theatre.

ೞ

"WHO IS THIS BRAZEN LITTLE UPSTART?" murmured the pillars of Dublin's theatre establishment as Deirdre O'Connell took up her mission to bring the theory and techniques of Constantin Stanislavsky to a new generation of Irish theatregoers. Marlon Brando personified all the mumbling and scratching torture of "The Method" and a large segment of Ireland's influential theatre people could not get past it.

"In the early 1960s," said Deirdre,

> "the prevailing idea in Dublin was that actors did not need to train. They were born and it had never been questioned that an actor didn't just get up and act. I, therefore, must have had impudence of the highest order, a cheeky upstart of barely twenty-three, to come over here and set up a studio to teach the Irish, who are born actors, how to act! Most people found it difficult to consider that actors must train like any other artist or craftsperson. That thought was anathema to them. It was either the actor has it or hasn't. The young Abbey, for example, was not so much a training process as a preparation-for-performance process, whereas the Stanislavsky system is a very precise systematic and gruelling, if rewarding, study of principles and practices. And that was the process they did not understand." (Interviewed by Joe Jackson, *Hot Press* Magazine, 1984).

And Deirdre goes on,

> "There had to be a reaction to this extreme situation and that
> is why Stanislavsky has been so successful. Otherwise, there
> would have been a mass exodus to London for there were no
> other opportunities to train in Ireland."

The Joe Jackson interview went on to analyse more deeply this
extreme and hostile reception:

> There may however have been a more direct political dimen-
> sion to the rejection of Stanislavsky's teachings. In Ireland in
> the early '60s, Deirdre's association with the German commu-
> nist, Erwin Piscator, who was director of the Dramatic Work-
> shop, can hardly have won her many friends and if it influ-
> enced people, it can only have been in a damagingly negative
> way. "I am very proud of my relationship with Erwin and I
> will never apologise for it. Apologise! Why should I? I bring
> up his name at every opportunity. But he'd been thrown out
> of America during the McCarthy witch-hunt and so my asso-
> ciation with him did ruffle the feathers of certain people here."

Undoubtedly, Deirdre's reception, in the inward-looking Ireland of the early 1960s, was distinctly unwelcoming. In pursuing
her naïve vision for a new and dynamic theatre in Ireland, she
had no earthly idea what she was dealing with. It takes some kind
of determination to follow your dream in the face of such seething
antipathy. A lesser mortal would have been paralysed.

However, not all voices were so scathing and Deirdre found a
good friend and ally in Ursula White Lennon, director of the aptly
named Pocket Theatre in Ely Place. Deirdre's plan was an ambitious one, considering she was twenty-three years of age, with very
little resources and few friends and was trying to break into a sus-
picious and discouraging environment. She wanted to train a permanent company of actors and directors under the Stanislavsky
method and eventually present the great classics at Ely Place.

Playwrights such as Chekhov and Ibsen, the pioneers of modern drama, inspired the Stanislavsky system. Their insightful exploration of intimate human relationships were at the heart of every theme they considered. The script, far from being neglected, comes into its own, fully substantiated and justified.

> The Stanislavsky system broke with the exhibitionist tendencies of nineteenth-century actor-managers and presented a new vision — theatre that depends on qualities of performance which emphasise and develop the non-verbal as well as the verbal aspects of theatre. A company, therefore, which has trained together, evolved an agreed language and standard of performance, and practises in the comparative peace of a studio atmosphere the difficult art of working co-operatively on stage, is in a particularly good position to realise these fundamental aspects and aspirations of modern theatre. (From the Dublin Focus Theatre Handbook.)

Deirdre's ambitious plan was derailed after the first production of Hermann Hesse's *Steppenwolf*, when the Pocket Theatre was sold for development and went the way of so many other small theatre venues at the time. Deirdre's fledging company had become homeless.

However, the skeleton of what would later become The Focus Theatre had now been formed with Deirdre as teacher, producer, director and actor. Her first students walked in off the street, announcing that they wanted to act. It touched a chord. Hadn't Deirdre done the very same in her previous life? Sabina Coyne, Tom Hickey, Timothy McDonnell, Frank McDonald, Johnny Murphy, Declan and Mary Elizabeth Burke-Kennedy, Meryl Gourley and Joan Bergin became the core of her new company and, though moving on to great heights of international success, each of them would return again and again to Focus as their spiritual home. This bond held tight over the next thirty-five years.

 CB

AFTER THE SUDDEN DEMISE of the Pocket Theatre, Deirdre and her Studio took up temporary residence at the Pike Theatre, but an itinerant existence such as this would never put flesh on her dream. She needed money, real money, to build a theatre of her own.

What was Dublin like in 1963? What was Ireland like? An abandoned child, dirty, grimy, shoeless and ragged. Boarded-up tenements tottering on the verge of collapse, broken footpaths and cratered roads, once-gracious Georgian homes now teetering like toothless and grizzled old men, smoke-clogged skies and blackened buildings, all grey and black and sad.

But that abandoned child was finding her feet and determinedly moving on.

Clutches of novice writers were meeting in cold and damp bed-sits on Leeson Street, labouring away on the great Irish novel. Songs of rebellion, long buried under Ireland's thin veneer of middle-class respectability, were unearthed and renewed in the back room of O'Donoghue's pub. Dublin's street ballads bounced back to life. Ireland was moving into the rebellious '60s in her own unique way.

Deirdre O'Connell could stop traffic. This was not London and she wasn't waving her hand, but she wafted down Leeson Street with an imperial grace, her red mane piled high, her capes and cloaks flapping in the wind, eyes fastened in front of her, lost in thought. Black was the colour she wore; flowing black skirts, black tights, black pumps and black shawls. Her only concession to the passing of time was the number of layers she put on. In summer, she removed a few; in winter she piled them thick. She tightly clutched her ever-present clipboard and script, and her bottomless black bag. She was naked without them.

Maureen O'Donoghue became her surrogate mother and Paddy her surrogate Dad.

Deirdre was renting a basement flat on Hatch Street and living on fresh air and food of the spirit. As her slight body got thinner and thinner, Maureen took to trying to fatten her up. It was a thankless job. A boiled egg, a slice of brown bread and a lump of cheese sustained her for most of her life. Food was lovely to look at and a mystery to taste. But Deirdre always had bigger things on her mind. Right now, the need was money and the goal was her own theatre. New York was too far and too expensive to reach. England would have to do.

Resolutely resurrecting her dormant singing career, she headed off to London, singing the songs of the protest generation in the workingmen's clubs of London and the North of England. She was staying in an Irish rooming house on Seven Sisters' Road in Finsbury Park, and it was there that she met Luke Kelly.

The attraction was instant, and terminal. Luke Kelly was a young Dubliner who had left home to follow the path of McAlpine's Fusiliers. His labouring on construction sites throughout the North of England had led him in a radical new direction, along the political road to socialism and the social-justice road to the music of Pete Seeger and Ewan McColl.

So alike were Deirdre and Luke, they could have been mistaken for brother and sister. The same flaming manes and the same searing fires in their souls. Luke, his leonine head thrown back with banjo strapped across his chest, that powerful, throaty voice raised in song; Luke telling the stories of the dispossessed, the deportee, the fettered, the used and abused, the truths of the working man. "With his halo of orange curls and his fine chiselled features, if he had landed in Peru, they would have taken him for an Aztec god," according to writer Ulick O'Connor. "He had the love of words and the precise elocution of the true Dubliner and when he sang he would caress the tempo of the lyric lovingly against the musical line, in a spine-tingling blend. . . . It was a compulsive sound, as if the harsh winds that snake up the Liffey had found their way into the human voice to emerge transformed by melody."

Beside him stood Deirdre, singing "The Three Marys" and "The Unquiet Grave", with all her intensity and her pain. Deirdre and

Luke. There they were, tramping up and down the smoke-clogged roads of industrial Britain, leading their own small rebellion.

But there was another side to this renegade pair. I see them now, in my mind's eye. It is long past midnight on a balmy summer's night and we are heading home after a noisy, boisterous singing gig, fish and chips and newspaper wrapper to hand; home to the flat we all share on Seven Sisters' Road. Luke's banjo, uncovered and strapped across his back, sandals and cords and open-necked shirt. Deirdre comes racing from behind, shawls flying, laughing and shouting and leaps up onto his back, clinging tight like a koala wrapped around a tree. Off they gallop down the road, two wild urchins loose on the streets of Finsbury Park.

Deirdre's regular trips back to Dublin kept the studio going and her bank balance growing. From 1964 through 1967, the Studio would perform weekly improvisations in the old Shakespeare Company in Fitzwilliam Square. "We would decide on a theme for the evening and two situations related to that theme," recounted Deirdre in an interview with Dave McKenna for *Magill* magazine. "We would then work out the relationships, circumstances and issues coming from that theme, undirected and unrehearsed. The audience would also play roles; a classroom of children, a TV audience or townspeople. Sometimes we'd run sequels and the audience kept coming back to follow the fortunes of a particular group of people. To see how a dramatic situation developed." These "improvs" were a "spectacular exhibition of the fruits of Stanislavsky's methods", according to theatre critic Dave McKenna in *Magill* magazine. But Deirdre was always on the lookout for a suitable permanent home, something intimate and accessible, something that could be tailored to fit her vision.

Luke had also returned to Dublin to join forces with a motley crew of bearded balladeers who met regularly in the small recesses of O'Donoghue's. Their Sunday afternoon sessions became infamous — Ronnie Drew contributing his raunchy street songs, Ciaran Bourke the tin whistle, John Sheahan on violin and Barney

McKenna the wizard on a banjo. This magical five had gelled into something approaching a working group, anarchic though it was and would forever remain. While Deirdre was in search of a theatre home, they were in search of a name. Following one particularly raucous music session in O'Donoghue's, the inevitable squabbling over possible names commenced. Luke looked up from the ubiquitous book in his hand and offered the obvious, the perfect resolution, "The Dubliners". James Joyce had won the day.

In 1963, the boys signed a contract with Transatlantic Records and recorded their first LP, entitled simply *The Dubliners*. With successful sales in Ireland and abroad, they went on to take the English folk cub scene by storm. Individually, they were superb musicians and performers, but collectively, they were dynamite, with a rough diamond quality that gripped an audience and held it fast. Their irreverence for all the established institutions of the time and their somewhat laconic view of themselves and Irish society in general encapsulated the tenor of an increasingly confident and rebellious generation.

 C3

IN 1964, TALLAGHT WAS A VILLAGE and the Embankment was its heartbeat. Mick McCarthy, a loquacious Kerryman, a gentleman and a scholar, was also the proprietor and burgeoning entrepreneur of the Embankment. He gave full rein to a stream of ballad groups emerging onto the vibrant Irish music scene, and chief among these was The Dubliners.

Another Dubliner, with the unlikely name of Alo Zakowski, became one of their first managers. Bookings had to be arranged and someone had to make sure the boys arrived where they were meant to be anywhere within an hour or so of the appointed time. Following what would always be a scintillating warm-up session at O'Donoghue's, Alo could be seen racing around Stephen's Green, organising taxis and shoving the boys, instruments, girlfriends, friends and various other hangers-on into taxis for the excursion out to Tallaght. Although the Embankment was no more than a big barn-like affair with wooden tables and chairs and a few microphones lined up along the stage, the vibrations inside were electric. A confident young Irish generation was coming of age and embracing all the liberating influences of the time. Deirdre and Luke were in the middle of all that.

The Clancy Brothers and Tommy Makem were big names on the folk music scene at the time and, although they were based in New York, they were also regular performers in Ireland. Liam and Tom Clancy in particular became great friends to Deirdre and Luke and often joined in rollicking all-night music sessions that spontaneously followed a successful Embankment gig. Initially, these sessions took place in their flat in Kenilworth Square and later on in their home at Dartmouth Square. They made music for the pure joy of it. Everyone and anyone could take the floor and every offering, ranging anywhere from playing the spoons to delivering dramatic recitations, was received with rapturous applause. It was also around this time that Liam gave Luke his first really good banjo.

But Deirdre developed a special friendship with Tom Clancy. He was the actor in the group and he had built a successful theatre career in New York long before the boys became household music names. Deirdre and Tom had a lot in common: New York, acting and the theatre. She spoke of him often and followed his career down through the years.

In 1965, there were two weddings in the O'Connell family. I married Tom Cusack, from County Cavan, whom I had met in the old Metropole Ballroom in Dublin. Following four years of working for BKS, I had decided to go back to New York and activate my teaching career. Tom followed and we were married on Easter Monday in the Church of the Blessed Sacrament in the Bronx. Two months later, Deirdre married Luke Kelly in the Church of the Holy Child in Whitehall, Dublin.

Tom and I had a small, traditional wedding, with those of my immediate family who were left in the Bronx in attendance and a telephone link with the Cusack family in County Cavan. Deirdre and Luke's wedding was as unconventional as their lives together would later be.

As brother Emmett recalls, "They were married in the summer of 1965 without an ounce of sense between the two of them. Since Dad was unable to travel to Dublin, Paddy O'Donoghue gave Deirdre away. I had to plead with Deirdre not to be married in all black. How could she expect Mom to understand that? As a compromise, she wore a white top to an otherwise simple black dress. For a wedding present, I bought a carload of groceries and stocked up their cupboard. Domestic and culinary arts were never Deirdre's strong points and both were as thin as whippets. They seemed to feed off an unquenchable source of internal energy that required little outside sustenance.

"With Luke earning the occasional big fee now and again, they kept an open house, unsuspecting and generous to a fault. . . . I can never think of one without the other. The two of them singing duets, with Deirdre perched on the arm of Luke's chair, was an experience to witness. The picture of Luke in his prime singing 'The Black and Amber Ale' and 'Joe Hill', with his head of tight curls thrown back, his eyes closed and his skinny legs quivering with energy is etched forever in my memory. Wise girl that she was, Deirdre never tried to upstage Luke or compete with his performance. Acting was her bowl of rice, singing was Luke's."

In order to keep the studio going, Deirdre continued to sing. Sometimes at the Embankment, or it could be the Gate Theatre, but most often it was "Midnight at the Grafton". That was an experience not to be missed for spectators who queued up for hours outside the Grafton Cinema for the privilege of barracking any troubadour impudent enough to take them on. This was not Deirdre's scene at all. She would have to find another way to finance her art.

She returned to New York four times over the next seven years to work in summer season productions with established repertory companies, earning the lucrative sums on offer to an actor of her calibre on the American stage. In 1967, studio members began a city-wide search for a suitable theatre premises. Declan Burke-Kennedy located an abandoned clothing labels factory at the end of a small, quiet mews off Pembroke Street. Declan and Deirdre entered into negotiations with the owners and three thousand pounds secured the lease. Deirdre emptied her entire savings of one thousand pounds and the remainder was made up by an un-named benefactor, whom everyone knew to be Luke. In 1967, this was an enormous sum of money, virtually everything they had between them.

With the unstinting support of Mick McCarthy and the firm of Burke-Kennedy Architects, plus an extraordinary level of volunteer labour from well-wishers and friends, this abandoned site became the 73-seater theatre that still exits today, and it was to become the womb that nourished and gave birth to scores of actors, directors, and new Irish playwrights whose work would otherwise never have seen the light of day. In August of 1967, Focus Theatre incorporating the Stanislavsky Studio opened its doors with Doris Lessing's "Play With a Tiger". It was an exhilarating, adrenaline-charged, earth-shattering moment for this little band of explorers of the mind. Bored Dublin barely blinked.

Deirdre was to return to New York for summer seasons again and again, arrive back in Dublin with deep pockets and proceed to plough every penny back into the Focus. Grants from the Arts Council were initially denied because she couldn't pay equity rates to her cast, even though the actors, designers, directors, stage managers and lighting crew were willing to work for the takings at the door. In latter years, the company received a sub-vention from the Council against losses, which at least helped to keep the doors open. Fees charged for the Stanislavsky Studio hardly changed over the years. Two to three pounds for up to six hours of work, and only charged to those who could pay. But the unyielding economics of running a theatre were to plague Deirdre's vision for the rest of her working life.

"I never intended to move into the mainstream of Irish theatre," said Deirdre.

> "From the beginning, I wanted to start a Stanislavsky-based company. By our constitution and structure, Focus is not and does not desire to be a platform for individual performers more concerned with their own careers than the artistic endeavours at hand. It is no surprise then, that the finest Focus productions have been noted for 'teamwork', and 'integrity' and for their clear sense of direction and their 'disciplined performances'. I felt that Dublin lacked an ever-present programme of international modern classical theatre and I was sure that Focus could fill that void." (From "Dublin Women in the Arts".)

ᛣ

WHILE DEIRDRE WAS EMBARKING on a lifetime of service to Irish theatre, Emmett had entered into partnership with Dublin architect Uinseann McEoin, and bought the publishing rights to several moribund Irish periodicals including *Development*, *Plan* and *Field and Stream*. As editor of *Development*, Emmett became a prolific commentator on current economic and political issues. In addition to three pamphlets, one of which presented a formidable case for a Federal Ireland, he had over one hundred political and economic articles published in Irish and American magazines and newspapers.

Emmett followed that venture with a relatively brief period trading in precious metals. His company, Numismatic Metals, became the only company in Ireland, outside of the four banking giants, licensed to trade in gold. He then turned his attentions to the ever-expanding world of oil and gas, exploring potential fields of activity from the mountain ranges of Colombia to the lush bayous of Louisiana and on to the frozen north of Russia.

Emmett's first oil and gas enterprise in Ireland was Eglinton Oil and Gas in Dublin, followed shortly by Osceola Explorations. Roisín was the first of three children born to Ray and himself, followed by Robert Emmett and Oisín. And by that time, Gretta was the only one of the South Bronx Five still living at home in the Bronx.

But Gretta had now discovered how to see the world in a way that she could afford. She became an air hostess with Pan American World Airlines. After an initial training period in Florida, she moved in with two colleagues to a trendy skyscraper apartment in midtown Manhattan and on her frequent trips home to Dublin she started appearing on Leeson Street in her spiffy flight uniform complete with jauntily tilted hat and black leather bag. Another reincarnation. Aunt Annette O'Connell walked again.

In 1972, Gretta married John Patrick Collins, a New Yorker and a Harvard graduate, in Our Lady of the Rosary Church in Greystones, County Wicklow. And in that same year, Mom and Dad sold everything they owned in the Bronx and moved back to retire in Bray. The circle was still revolving and in constant motion.

It is often an impossible and thankless venture, this return to the homeland after a lifetime away. So many dreams are built in the deep recesses of the mind, but cold reality has a way of dashing them viciously into dust.

It was always going to be an uneasy truce between Mom and Dad, this coming home. Mom's world was in the Bronx. She was a warm and gentle woman with a wild innocence, one who could find good in the blackest of knaves. Family came above all else. She looked forward to the weekly visits from her sisters, the cups of tea with the neighbours and the daily rounds of shopping, cooking and sewing. She didn't want to leave all that was dear and strike out once again into the unknown. She had returned to Ireland only once in all those years. To her, it was a foreign land. She loved Ireland as the home she had left. But her true loyalties were to America.

Dad was a man of dreams and the world is a lonely place for the likes of him. He was an intelligent, thoughtful and private man with unyielding principles. Like so many of his contemporaries, life had denied him his true potential. Life had got in the way. Yet, during all those years in New York, he had kept his eye fixed on his distant star. He had left Ireland against his will. He would eventually return to his home.

The fact that Emmett and Deirdre were already in Ireland made the move easier for Mom, and although I was still teaching in the Bronx it was my plan to return to Ireland with my husband and children as soon as we had saved up enough to put a down-payment on a house.

The Ireland that Mom and Dad returned to in 1972 was a society floundering between dependence and independence. The twenty-six-county Irish Free State had declared itself a republic in 1948, but more than fifty years after the Easter Rising, the Republic of Ireland's economy was still bound to the economy of Britain. The Irish punt was tied to sterling, pound for pound. Unemployment and emigration were again on the rise. There could be no political independence without economic freedom, reasoned Dad

As for the EEC, that was a European notion. It was difficult enough for those who had never left Ireland to get their heads around that impending development, never mind for someone who had just returned after spending forty years in the United States.

In the North of Ireland, British armed forces held sway over large sections of the six occupied counties. The British Government had introduced internment without charge or trial for suspected members of the IRA. Section 31 of the Irish Broadcasting Act of the Irish Republic enforced a blanket censorship over all statements from the leaders of Sinn Fein. What had happened to the glorious visions of the men and women of 1916? Where should his loyalties lie now?

Dad continued to read and he started to brood. Not wanting to disillusion his American-born children who had also come home to make their lives in Ireland, he suffered his disappointments in silence.

cs

GRETTA AND PATRICK BEGAN their married life in a one-bedroom brownstone apartment in fashionable mid-Manhattan, where Patrick worked for a corporate law firm. Patrick, who was given to beginning his working day by throwing open the bedroom window and roaring out to an unsuspecting public, "Good Morning, America! I'm mad as hell and I'm not gonna take it any more", was not corporate life material. So he and Gretta upped sticks and headed off for the new frontier in the far reaches of Oklahoma. Patrick had also been bitten by the exploration bug and, disregarding the uncertain politics of the time, he started up an oil and gas company to explore new fields in the south and west of the United States. Their daughter Courtney was born in Lake Aluma, Oklahoma in 1980. Deirdre shocked everyone by flying off to New York and travelling on by Greyhound Bus to become one of Courtney's godparents, along with Patrick's business partner, Billy Hitchcock.

That was the only occasion on which Deirdre left Focus for any extended period. Her theatre, her studio and her actors had come to consume her life, and the few acres from her home at Dartmouth Square, along the Grand Canal and down Leeson Street had become her sacred patch.

Deirdre had always been a bad traveller, preferring to walk everywhere. She would only get into a car if there were no other alternative. Rain or shine, snow or sleet, she could be seen floating along Leeson Street to her destination, the Focus. But as the years went by, she developed a mortal fear of flying, which was one of the reasons why she stayed so close to home.

Technologically, she was useless, barely able to find the button on an electric kettle. As for computers, well, in her own words, "I wouldn't know what to do with one if it jumped up and bit me on the nose." While television held no attraction for her, she was addicted to the radio, and it could be heard playing round the clock at her home in "The Dart".

But following Courtney's christening in Oklahoma, Deirdre took to the roads. She boarded a Greyhound Bus in Oklahoma and headed off alone on a most unlikely adventure, her first stop being the sun-baked world of the Aztecs. That must have been some sight, Deirdre wrapped in her black woollen skirts and shawls meandering through the white-washed and winding streets of Santa Fé, American's "Land of Enchantment", with adobe huts and Indian turquoise all around her.

Kevin had always been attracted to the southwest and, after serving for twenty years with the New York City Police Department, he and Kathy and family had moved on to start a new life in Texas. He remained in the United States Army Reserve for the rest of his working life, attached to Army Intelligence, and to his everlasting pride, their eldest son, Liam, became a West Point Army cadet. The issue of divided loyalties had never entered this picture.

So a visit with Kevin, Kathy and family in the hill country of Austin, Texas, became Deirdre's next interlude. But for her, peaceful relaxation could only be taken in small doses. It wasn't long before she was on the road again, this time heading for San Antonio with its fabled river walks and Mexican Mariachi bands. New Orleans was to be her final destination.

If Deirdre had not been so rooted in Dublin, I believe she would have found a spiritual home in New Orleans. This was her sort of place and her kind of people. From the sweltering bayous to the rolling Mississippi, from the opulence of Royal Avenue to the swinging French Quarter, among trumpeters and drummers and artists and down-and-outs, Deirdre was instantly at home.

Gardens of good and evil flourished in this intriguing place and she loved all of it. Many years later, in her home at "The Dart", she was still receiving cards and messages from the innkeepers and stall-keepers, and the shopkeepers and street people whom she had befriended along the way.

CB

DURING THE EARLY YEARS OF OUR MARRIAGE, Tommy and I shared a two-family house in the Bronx with my parents, and I went back there to teach in what had become the Puerto Rican barrios of the South Bronx. I clearly remember the strange sensation that overcame me, as I looked out the window of my sixth-grade classroom and into the back garden of our old home on East 139th Street. Shattered glass windows were encased in iron bars, the highly polished back door was cracked and broken and covered in graffiti, and Romeo and Juliet had decayed into a lump of brown rust, strangled by a maniacal jungle of weeds. None the less, the tough little rosebush that we had dug from the ruins of Mom and Dad's home in Banteer still scrambled over the back wall, blooming in what had become a wasteland. Hope springs eternal out of ruins such as these.

The old neighbourhood had changed, changed utterly. Now the schoolteachers were black and white, Jewish and Christian, Italian and Irish. And all the students were Hispanic and Black Americans.

Mabel Kennedy, Principal of PS 43 on Brown Place, hand-picked her teachers and trained them in her own image. Here was a principal from the old school. The severely fastened, grey hair bun and the thick-soled, flat shoes went hand in glove with "old-fashioned" ideas about respect and commitment to the teaching profession. In a public school that had security guards posted on all doors, she enforced a code of discipline and respect that neighbouring schools could only dream of. Her enforcer was Joe Edwards.

Mr Edwards was a coal-black Jamaican and a six-foot four-inch powerhouse. He was also a former member of the United States Marine Corps. Joe Edwards was Mabel Kennedy's Deputy Principal and every teacher's hero.

I had done my practice teaching in PS 43 as a twenty-year-old student at Notre Dame. Now I was back. I was in awe of Joe Edwards and in mortal fear of Miss Kennedy. There was a time clock in the main office for punching in. Punch in late, and you got a pink slip. Three pink slips and you were out the door, never to darken it again.

Teachers met their students in the outdoor schoolyard every morning, rain or shine. The first bell rang and classes lined up in their designated places, teachers at the head of the lines and students standing one head behind the other. The second bell rang and Mr Edwards appeared, walking up and down the lines, patting coat and pants pockets and checking for concealed weapons. When the third bell rang, the classes filed quietly into the school building. Doors were locked behind them.

Security guards were there to keep the parents out, not to keep the students in. Drugged-up or enraged parents were a real threat, so officers escorted visitors from the entrance to the main office where the secretary interviewed them about the purpose of the visit. Then, either she gave them a classroom pass to proceed with the visit, or the officer re-escorted to them to the exit. The protection of both students and staff was top priority.

My first class was a conglomeration of repeat students ranging in age between thirteen and fifteen; after my first term of teaching, I had developed a nervous twitch. I couldn't hold my head still. I was an emotional and physical wreck.

The girls in my class were far, far worse than the boys and the abuse they hurled at one another and at the teachers was horrendous. I was called, "You white motherfucker" so often, I was in danger of thinking it was part of my name. These girls were fuelled by an anger that knew no bounds. The conditions in which they lived were steeped in poverty, drug and alcohol abuse and sexual exploitation. They were the victims of it all.

But the boys posed a real physical threat. Knives and home-made zip-guns were as common as the *Daily News*. One day, one of my most orderly and diligent students drew a six-inch kitchen knife on the boy sitting behind him because that boy had looked at his paper. After retrieving the knife and calming the would-be assailant down, I sent the class monitor running for Mr Edwards. Miguel was removed from class and a message went home asking a parent to come to school. No details of the incident were released.

The next day, Mr Ruiz appeared at my door with his classroom pass all in order. I stepped outside the classroom, with Miguel, and began to explain what had happened the previous day. As I was speaking, Mr Ruiz calmly began to remove his pants belt and then he wrapped it around his fist. I watched in horror as he ordered Miguel onto his knees in front of me and began whipping the child around his head with the belt buckle.

My screams stunned Mr Ruiz to a halt and brought Mr Edwards racing down the hall. Mr Ruiz was baffled. Hadn't his son misbehaved in school? Hadn't he humiliated his father? Hadn't he the right, and, yes, the duty as a god-fearing man to chastise his son? This is what he was doing. He was demonstrating to me, the teacher, his total respect. And he was beating his son into obedience. I had learned a valuable lesson. Cultural differences could be as wide as an ocean and until I understood them better, I would not send for a parent again.

Russell Burnwell was an intriguing young man of fifteen; tall, handsome and charming, and possessing a silver tongue. He put that particular gift to good use as a storefront preacher in the army of the Lord. He would regularly stay back after school to practise his sermons in front of me, polishing up his delivery and interjecting joyous "Hallelujahs!" and "A-A-A-mens" at just the right points. I was an enthusiastic cheerleader, overjoyed as I was to witness such youthful devotion in the midst of social disintegration. All was going swimmingly until one day Mr Edwards appeared at my classroom door with two police detectives in tow.

"Hey, Mon! Get your black ass up here, now, you son of a black bastard," roared Joe Edwards, glaring down the aisle at the pious Russell cowering in his seat. And when Russell didn't haul ass quick enough, why old Joe Edwards just about strangled him with his necktie and dropped him at the feet of the detectives. I was stupefied. Had the amazing Mr Edwards just lost it? What did he think he was doing, manhandling my star pupil?

They promptly escorted Russell out of the classroom, out of the building and into a waiting patrol car. It seems my charming Mr Burnwell was all things to all people; as well as God's preacher, he was the local fence for stolen property and his store-front church was a very convenient blind. He had managed all of that at the age of fifteen. He could have set the world on fire. Instead, he had "roasted his ass" and ended up in reform school.

I survived that year and, notwithstanding the nervous twitch, I became a permanent teacher on Miss Kennedy's staff. The following year, in recognition of my baptism of fire, I was given the top fourth-grade class and fell in love with my ten-year-old students and with the art of teaching. This was the same school in the same neighbourhood and all my students were black and Puerto Rican angels. I was their teacher but clearly, I still had a lot to learn.

cs

OUR DAUGHTERS, GERALDINE ANN AND AISLING, were born in the Bronx and we moved back to Ireland the year following my parents' departure. We bought a home in what was then the newly developing suburb of Malahide and I went back to work in a boys' national school in Kilbarrack. Sadly, following the birth of our third daughter, Breifní, my Mom's health began to fail, so Mom and Dad left their home in Bray and moved in with us. And despite all, Dad never lost his vigour to fight. Whenever Breifní began to cry, for whatever reason, Dad would encourage her to keep on yelling. "Go on, sweetheart, yell as loud as you can. Protest! Learn to protest!" And he continued to sprinkle those infant wails with grains of optimism and hope.

Our Mom passed away on the 28th of January 1978 and Dad went into a rapid decline from the minute she went into the ground. Though we always believed that Dad was a man of steel and head of the house, in the end we discovered that it was Mom who had been his heart and his soul and his strength. And he was not able to carry on without her. With the heart of a forty-year-old man and every vital organ in his body healthy, he died less than a year later. He died from a broken heart. Nellie and Michael Joe are buried together in St Peter's Cemetery in Little Bray.

Four generations of emigration and return, of fractured cultures and divided loyalties went into that grave. But they did not find rest. The struggle that had begun a century earlier in Cork and Galway and Sligo had penetrated the life blood of the Taaffe-O'Connell family, and would direct the paths of many, many lives for generations to come.

The death of both parents within so short a space of time had a profound effect on all of us. Though we were raised at a time and in a place that had been a hotbed of potential doom, we always knew that Nellie and Michael Joe had a wisdom that went far beyond school learning. They were wise in the ways of the spirit and they gave us to believe that all things were possible.

☙

Chapter 8

LEARNING TO FLY

IT WOULD APPEAR that all Americans are drawn, in one way or another, to the story of the American Indian. Although we, of the "first generation", sometimes had difficulty defining ourselves, and our national identities, we certainly knew all about Indians. It is part of the national consciousness or, one might say, part of the national psychosis. Knowing that great injustices have been done to a whole race of people, and have never been undone, is a deeply troubling thing.

During the time when we had been performing with the Bob Barrett School of Irish Dancing at parish events throughout New York City, we had taken part in a fund-raising concert for a group of Pueblo Indian boys who were studying at Manhattan College in the Bronx. Several of those boys became our lifetime friends. Years later, after having completed my college degree, and partly as result of that friendship, I had applied to the Federal Bureau of Indian Affairs for a teaching position with the Pueblo Indian Tribe of New Mexico.

All applications for more than 200 American Indian tribes had to go through a central clearinghouse in Albuquerque. The application process was a long and arduous one and Native Americans, those who held officially registered tribal numbers, received first preference. Consequently, my application had run on for several years. In the meantime, I had moved back to Ireland with

Tommy and the children and was teaching in Malahide. Tommy had started up his own cement business.

However, the worldwide financial upheaval created by the oil crisis of the early 1970s had contributed to a worsening economic climate in Ireland. Then, in the latter part of the decade, rising political tensions on the island exploded. Northern Ireland was in flames. Unemployment stood at 10 per cent in the Republic. Thousands of ordinary people from both North and South headed for the emigrant queues. Some were legal. Many more just slipped by.

Tommy's fledgling cement business fell victim to the times. He left for London and that which had begun as a temporary solution became the pattern of our lives for many years to come. Short-term emigration to England or Scotland to find work, followed by sudden reappearances when funds were replenished, had been a familiar way of life for generations of Irish families. But combined with this uncertain lifestyle was Tommy's mercurial nature. He made serious decisions with lightning speed. He was not one for long explanations. Circumstances dictated action. Long explanations served no purpose other than delay. The reasons for action were meant to be telepathically understood.

I had a long talk with myself and decided that it was no use trying to change the flow of the tide or the will of a man. Nature would prevail. We could carry on as we were doing for years, and we would survive, but the future for our girls looked bleak. Bargain-basement selling was not what I had in mind for any of them. There had to be alternative ways to make a life in this world. It was just a case of finding them. And although, no doubt, they would be unconventional, they would probably be none the worse for that. With a bit of luck, they could even be better.

It was not easy, in the beginning, but we got better and better at it, with time and practice. It was a bit like going back and learning to play the violin all over again. You have to find the exact spot on the string to place your finger in order to avoid the screech.

We decided to rent out our house in Malahide for a few years and we left for America with five suitcases and three young daughters. We had no definite plan but we had good health, good educations, three healthy children and an American passport. I figured that, all things considered, we were way ahead of the pack. In addition, I had one more big advantage. I had renewed contact with the Federal Bureau of Indian Affairs and I was full of hope that an imminent job offer would be in the post.

It was. Two weeks after arriving in the United States, an offer dropped through the letter box in Malahide and was forwarded on to my Aunt Annette in Florida. The clearinghouse in Albuquerque had finally accepted my application and had passed it on to headquarters in Washington, DC. However, the position that I was being offered was not with the Pueblo Indians, as I had hoped, but with a radical new bilingual education project being formulated by the Seminole Tribe of Florida.

I had never before heard of the Seminole Tribe. Comanches, Cherokees, Apaches, Hopi, Sioux and Mohawks were all familiar names to me. But Seminoles? I was soon to discover that 2,000 men, women and children made up the Seminole Tribe of Florida.

During the late 1940s, a team of United States Army engineers had arrived in Florida with a mission. It was to clear the steaming swamplands of America's southeast and make them habitable for human life. The engineers embarked on a staggering project of land reclamation. They drained tens of thousands of acres of swampland, rerouted the natural flow of the massive Kissimmee River and created hundreds of miles of water canals for crop irrigation. In the process, they also managed to uncover a thriving but long-forgotten piece of American history.

A band of people who looked like they had just stepped out from the pages of history emerged from the swamps. The men were dressed in multicoloured fringed skirts and buckskin leggings. They wore beaded armlets and carried intricately decorated shot pouches across their shoulders. They had knives and blow-

pipes strapped across their chests. The women wore heavily lay-
ered flowing skirts covered by filmy capes. Older women piled
their thick black hair high and swept it back over a board, which
was shaped like the brim of a hat. Young women wore their hair
flowing freely down their backs, with rows and rows of beaded
necklaces reaching nearly to their waists. They were the descendants of a ragged band of Indians from Alabama and Georgia,
who had eluded capture by the United States Army during the
dying days of the Seminole Wars.

In 1858, at the conclusion of the three Seminole Wars, the
Seminole Tribe had rejected a peace treaty with the United States
Government that would have transported them forcibly to the
Arkansas territory. Thousands of Seminoles were killed during
the wars and a few hundred were captured. The vanquished Indians were marched one thousand miles along the "Trail of Tears"
to reservations in Arkansas and Oklahoma. A small number had
escaped into the alligator-infested waters of the Everglade
swamps, a place where they knew no white man would ever follow them.

That band of Indians had not only survived, but had multi-
plied, and they emerged into post-World War II America as
though time had stood still.

The United States Government agreed to recognise this rem-
nant band of Seminoles as an official tribe and in the year 1957, 862
registered members were incorporated into the Seminole Tribe of
Florida. Their territorial jurisdiction included 42,000 acres of reservation lands around the Big Cypress Swamp. Although they never
signed a peace treaty with the United States and are the only Indian tribe officially still "at war", they were eventually subsumed
under the governance of the Federal Bureau of Indian Affairs.

It was on Big Cypress Reservation, among the Seminole Indians, that my girls and I found a people whose history, at first
glance, seemed light years away from our own experience. Upon
reflection, we discovered a people with whom we shared similar

historical memories and spiritual forces, and the same painful crises of identity.

Tribal leaders had established camps at three different locations on reservation lands in order to accommodate distinct clan and language groupings. These were Brighton (Creek), Big Cypress (Miccosukee) and Hollywood (mixed). I was assigned to the new bilingual project that was being launched at Ahfachkee Day School on Big Cypress.

The community at this camp numbered four hundred men, women and children. Miccosukee was their language and it was an oral language only. Alarmingly, due to the powerful influences of radio and television and the growing interaction between reservation and outside communities, the native language was in imminent danger of disappearing. Elders, who spoke only Miccosukee, could no longer communicate with their grandchildren, who spoke mainly English. Seminole children were being educated through English in state public schools and they were absorbing the cultural identity that surrounded them. The psychological confusion brought on through loss of identity and the ensuing divided loyalties that accompany cultural change was already starting to creep into reservation life.

Critically, elders were the keepers of all tribal culture, history and medicine. If the tribe failed to codify the Miccosukee language and transcribe their oral history before the elders passed away, the unique identity and culture of Big Cypress Seminoles would be lost forever.

I had done postgraduate study in curriculum development at Hunter College in New York some years earlier, while at the same time teaching in the Bronx. My work had been in the area of minority cultures. This, along with my experience of teaching in a country where the first language, Gaeilge, was of no monetary value but, nonetheless, was compulsory in all state schools, was of special interest to the Seminole Tribe. They offered me a curriculum development position on the bilingual project and agreed that I would be able to take my daughters to live on the reservation with me. They would be educated along with the Native American children at Ahfachkee Day School. This was a huge concession. They were the first and only non-Indians to attend the reservation school.

The one disappointing feature in the offer was the stipulation that, while Tommy could live with us on the reservation, he could not work there; Indian preference prevailed. Neither of us was keen on the idea of him becoming a "trailing spouse" — that is, a non-working one. So after a fruitless search for suitable employment in the South Florida area, he decided to return to London where he still had contacts.

I could have insisted that he stay in Florida but it would have been pointless and divisive. This was going to be an exciting time for the girls, living on the reservation, and Tommy would be back for Christmas and the long summer holidays. Sometimes, circumstances arise that you have to look at in different ways, twist them around, examine them from different angles, and somehow make them work. To me, making life work is what life is all about.

❧

BIG CYPRESS RESERVATION is only seventy-five miles northwest of the play land that is Fort Lauderdale, but a million miles away from mainstream America. The most common name on Big Cypress is Osceola, after the legendary and heroic young warrior who had died in a United States military prison in 1837. Curiously, however, there were also a large number of Seminole males named both Jesse and Emmet. When I began to travel west to work with bilingual projects on Apache and Cheyenne reservations, I discovered the same phenomenon. What was the reason for this American Indian affinity for two very non-Indian Anglo names, I wondered?

All was revealed at a Native American workshop I attended in Winnipeg, Manitoba, where I had met yet another Indian Emmet.

He explained that such a sense of mystery could only exist in the mind of an Anglo. In fact, to an Indian, it made perfect sense.

Jesse James and Emmet Dalton had been the leaders of America's most notorious outlaw gangs in the early days of the Wild West — the James Gang and the Dalton Brothers. Any outlaw of the American Government had to be a hero to an American Indian. That reminded me of the old Irish adage about England's misfortune being Ireland's opportunity.

Reservation life turned out to be simple and self-contained. We lived in a three-bedroom aluminium trailer home surrounded by dense clumps of drooping cypress trees, one of which was home to a huge, wide-eyed and eerie-sounding barn owl. A very strange encounter with that bird brought us into close contact with hundreds of years of deeply buried Indian memory, and an Indian identity deeply scarred by the now familiar ravages of European invasion, colonisation, dislocation and acculturation . . .

Big Cypress steamed beneath a pale yellow moon and sultry skies loomed over its dark expanse. Thick clumps of reeds and cypress knees jutted out from the stagnant waters of its seething swamp, the murky surface disturbed only by rustles from a skulking alligator. Geckos darted through the night and bull frogs croaked in a festering pond. Swaying malallucas peeled off their paper barks like rattlers shedding their skins. In her aluminium-sided trailer home, Peggy David lay heavy with sleep on a suffocating slab of foam mattress, drugged as she was from the heat and sodden air. A limp mosquito net draped around her bed like a flimsy coffin.

Against the rim of the moonlit sky the brooding eyes of a reservation barn owl bore down on that home. This powerful bird sat as a solitary sentry atop a towering cypress tree. Peggy shuddered and shifted uneasily. More than the sweltering heat disturbed her sleep.

She drew her knees up, putting space between her sweating legs and the clammy foam that sucked her down into a pulsating pit. The soft drone of a ceiling fan crooned. She slipped back into the simmering night.

Estiginee-ee-ee
Estiginee-ee-ee

From somewhere deep within, Peggy's restless soul stirred. Still those baleful eyes bore down piercing through centuries of steely strength, centuries of visions, dreams, drums and dances. The spirits of the great and the good, the old and the aged, swelled up within her and burst forth. Peggy shot up.

Estiginee-ee-ee
Estiginee-ee-ee

The owl had not stirred from his perch but his familiar hoot had taken on the unspeakable screech of the evil spirit. Panic pounded in Peggy's head and in her heart. She knew that the spirit of the Estiginee stalked her from that tree, more fearsome, more frightful and more terrifying than all the panthers that prowled the teeming swamp.

There he sat, a bird of prey with the soul of a warped old man. A man, old and evil. An old man and an evil man who knows Indian medicine and can use that medicine to turn himself into an owl. That man-owl will then put himself outside the house of the young girl he covets. His chilling call and demonic gaze, his eyes — pools of debauchery — will paralyse his prey in her sleep. He will then enter her room and she will know she has been taken by the spirit of darkness when she awakes to find scratches from his talons on her hands.

Peggy had held these mysteries buried deep in her heart. She was a schoolteacher. She had a college degree. And she was a Seminole.

Every day Peggy worked, lived and played in the white man's world. Her smart red Trans-Am sped along Snake Road, top down, her charcoal hair snapping around her face. Genesis, the new man, born to the reservation but reared to the town, sat by her side.

Peggy raised the corners of the mosquito net, slipped out of bed, and crept across the room. The Estiginee's brooding silhouette filled her window and the night. As she stood rooted to the floor he turned his force fully upon her. His evil call washed over her and dragged her down, strangling her soul. Terror wracked her sweating body. The vulture tracked the sparrow.

> *Estiginee-ee-ee*
> *Estiginee-ee-ee*

Learned facts from learned books were of little use to Peggy now. The Estiginee's howl had unlocked her Indian past. Songs and stories of her childhood flooded her frenzied mind. Stories of forces fiercer than the roar of the sea and the fury of the wind. Forces that once unleashed would savage all in their path. Forces bred from bad medicine by one bound to evil. Forces of medicine and evil bonded soul to soul.

"The Estiginee enters where the spirit sleeps. Be aware, be awake, be on guard." Grandmother Nanno's words filled her consciousness. For a very long time, that wizened but wise old face had held no meaning for Peggy. She had moved on. The reservation Indian was but a dim and dull memory of a buried past. She was a modern, assimilated Indian, one who travelled easily in the white man's world.

But lessons of childhood are not easily forgotten, forever etched as they are on the soul. Discarded, perhaps, but not forgotten. Misplaced, but not forgotten.

Peggy stretched beneath the iron bedstead and silently withdrew her rifle. "More debris from the distant past," she thought. Even on this stifling summer's night, its steel barrel was cold to her touch. She eased it up, propped the butt against her shoulder and aimed.

"Go away," she shouted in a voice strained with fear. "Leave me in peace, Estiginee. I am not afraid of you! I will watch until dawn rises and you will be gone."

Peggy's grip tightened on the cold, hard steel and she fired. The blast slammed her sideways. She had aimed high. She must show the Estiginee that his power had not cowed her but she also knew that she dared not hit this man-owl. If shot, he would drop to the ground and owl would once again be man. If killed, his evil would disperse, invading the worlds of her family and friends. These old ways had simmered steadily beneath the surface of the new Indian.

She watched and waited, the chilling evil cry sweeping over chickees and swamps like a suffocating smog. With morning's first light, she bolted for Ahfachkee's schoolhouse.

There was no work done at Ahfachkee that day. Teachers and students alike were engrossed in the story of the Estiginee. Our trailer home sat right beside Peggy's, so Geraldine Ann, Aisling and Breifní were gripped with terror. What if the Estiginee turned his attentions on them? But no, that couldn't happen, they were assured. The power of the Estiginee reached only to Indians. And even though these girls might act like Indians, and think like Indians, they most definitely were not Indians.

All the school staff, from the principal down to the cleaners, were engulfed in the drama and they persuaded Peggy to go to Josie Billie. As the most respected Medicine Man of the tribe, he was the only person now who could help.

Josie had been born on a night when the skies had turned black, maybe ninety years before, maybe more. He had been one of the original band of Seminoles who had emerged from the swamps in 1948.

Josie listened as Peggy stumbled through her story, struggling with a language long lost to her tongue. His watery eyes squinted in his creased and weathered face and Peggy's tense frame eased in the light of his frail presence. Stacks of plants and roots ringed his hut and a low-banked fire smouldered like an eternal flame.

Josie's cracked and leathery fingers plucked bits of twigs and plants and pounded them into a dusty compound, which he rolled into a scrap of cloth. He then tied it firmly and placed it close to Peggy's heart. Chanting softly, he faced east, then west, north, then south, drawing Peggy slowly and hypnotically into his sacred circle. Her halting tongue followed his ancient chants, the murmuring sounds her succour and her strength.

Josie told Peggy to place the sachet of medicine under her mattress and to continue the chants every day at dawn until the screeching stopped. And for the next few days, we were awakened to the sound of Peggy's soft voice, murmuring the words of comfort as the morning sun *began to rise. The barn owl remained on his perch. But his familiar "hoot" returned and, with it, peace was restored to Ahfachkee.*

Peggy eventually moved on to another reservation in Oklahoma and when Geraldine Ann and I were clearing out her trailer in preparation for a new arrival, we found the patched sachet under her mattress. We left it where we found it. Peggy's fractured psyche was all tied up in that little patch of cloth; her clouded vision and her divided loyalties. It is never wise to tamper with things you do not fully understand.

಄

TERESA OSCEOLA JUMPER was, and is today, a remarkable woman. She became my friend and indispensable workmate on the bilingual education project. The project would have started up and perhaps stumbled along for a time, but without Teresa it would have quickly hit a solid wall of silence and collapsed.

Teresa was born on Big Cypress and raised in a Miccosukee-speaking family, in a traditional camp that comprised a collection of palm-thatched chickee huts. She was different in the sense that she was one of the few Big Cypress Seminoles who had completed high school education in Clewiston, 45 miles away. She was different in another sense too. She could see the value in preserving the essentials of Seminole life — its language, religion and medicine and not just the visual trappings of woven baskets, fine beadwork and alligator wrestling. She also realised that it would take work and time to make the Miccosukee language project a success.

Teresa and I drew up a plan for the programme. It would initially mean collecting information about Seminole history, clan life and traditional medicine, in Miccosukee, and on tape. Local legends could come at a later stage. I outlined the broad themes that we would consider and Teresa filled in the specific topics.

We then began to visit the camps of reservation elders every day, but we often came away with nothing. Teresa was able to sense when the elders were not ready to speak. So we would sit there in the chickee in silence, our hands quietly folded, with Teresa and her aunt or uncle gently nodding and murmuring softly. And then, just as quietly, we would withdraw — and wait for another time.

And in their own good time, the old people did relate what we needed. We then had to set about finding someone to help us transpose the oral into the written. That was my job and I found a willing accomplice in a most unlikely place, at the extreme edge of the continent, in Anchorage, Alaska. A truly enigmatic linguist from the Pacific Island of Tonga, Dr Tupou Pulu, had applied for and received federal funds to set up the National Bilingual Materials Development Center of Alaska to assist tribes, such as the Seminoles, to develop their written languages.

The school principal's family, kind and generous non-Indians from South Dakota, and two Seminole teacher aides volunteered to look after Geraldine Ann, Aisling and Breifní so that Teresa and I could avail of the centre's expert help. I was then able to travel contentedly, knowing that the children were in good hands.

Teresa and I arrived in Alaska in February of 1979 on the day that the dog sled races from Fairbanks were crossing the finishing line in Anchorage. It was fourteen degrees below zero, Fahrenheit. Teresa, a native of the steaming Florida swamps, accepted her down-filled snow suits with sombre equanimity and immediately set about the business of finding out how to write Miccosukee.

Several trained linguists worked with individuals from a number of different tribes. They listened, then repeated, then wrote. They developed these new written languages by using the basic Roman alphabet and then introducing newly constructed symbols for each tribe's unique sounds.

When Teresa felt she had mastered her new alphabet, which didn't take her very long, she began transposing the simplest of our tapes. The linguist was always beside her, on hand and ready to assist, but Teresa was the driving force. She would then pass both the English and the new Miccosukee versions of the piece on to me. It was an incredible sensation, looking at the written word where just days before there had been nothing.

I would then work with the linguist and Teresa to reword or rephrase the piece, and when we were all satisfied that the meaning was correct in both languages, we would hand them on to a Native American artist. Her job was to illustrate the pieces and return them to Teresa for authentication, or revisions whenever necessary. I would eventually receive the finished work and set about designing detailed lesson plans for the Miccosukee speaking teacher aides who would be responsible for delivering the lessons back on Big Cypress.

The work continued when we returned to the reservation three weeks later. We had completed the rough draft of one small booklet before we left Anchorage and we intended to use that as our guide for the future. We also engaged a local artist, Jo North, to give the work an even more authentic Seminole appeal.

Teresa and Jo moved slowly and spoke softly, and they spoke only when they had something worthwhile to say. Like most American Indians, they didn't believe in filling up silences with idle chatter. We often sat, side by side, in the quiet of our small library, poring over the new and unfamiliar shapes and trying to make sense out of what often looked like nonsense, for hours on end, without speaking a single word.

They never made sharp or jarring movements. They never made noise. All of their body parts seemed to move in perfect harmony. I could sometimes feel myself falling into a kind of hypnotic trance, lulled into space by a sense of total peace and quiet camaraderie.

Our work moved along at a steady pace and by the time I was ready to leave Big Cypress, we had revisited Anchorage with our rough drafts and had a series of six basic Miccosukee/English readers in the pipeline. Several additional Miccosukee teacher aides were in the process of being trained to work under the able supervision of Teresa and Jo.

☙

THE CHILDREN SPENT THEIR DAYS hunting in the woods for swamp apples, collecting fossils, and running from wild boars. They learned to speak the Miccosukee language while carving wooden implements and sewing patchwork skirts with elders under the cypress trees. They went to rodeos and turkey shoots, ate pit-barbequed deer, and joined in the Green Corn Dance. They were as much a part of reservation life as their friends, Rita Billie and Jason Tigertail.

We had an exchange programme on the reservation with children from the nearest state school in Clewiston, which was forty-five miles away. Primary school children would spend a day at Ahfachkee as guests of our students in the hope that familiarity would encourage a better understanding of the Indian way of life. But the Indians really hated it. They felt they were under a microscope, strange insects being gaped at by nosy strangers, strangers who were no different from the ones who had trampled through their lives and stolen their lands and their freedoms for hundreds of years. This feeling ran deep among elders and children alike. Yet, despite these feelings of suspicion and mistrust, they coveted all the trappings and playthings of the strangers' world.

The students from Clewiston didn't see it that way at all. They were genuinely interested in the native way of life and wanted to make friends with the Indians. Unfortunately, their sense of history was more than a bit skewed. They never did see the wrong that had been done. So, though they tried, they were up against a wall of silence they did not understand.

When they entered the three-room schoolhouse at Ahfachkee, each visitor took his place beside one of the Indian students. The hope was noble, that by the end of the day Indians and Anglos would be friends. The reality was vastly different. American Indians are a notoriously reserved people at the best of times. On such occasions, they were tight-lipped. Absolutely silent.

On one such occasion, a very chatty young visitor was seated beside Aisling and he tried valiantly, in every way he could, to open up a conversation with her. Aisling was a very non-Indian, red-haired paleface. But she was having none of it. Following the lead of the rest of her classmates, she resolutely ignored her white desk companion, rebuffing every attempt he made to be friendly. Eventually, the youngster had had enough and he busted out in a torrent of frustration. "Looka here, girl. Why ain't ya'll talkin' to me? Y'all ain't Indian. Y'all white, jest like me." Aisling's Indian friend, Charlie Cypress, was sitting on the other side of her. Without raising his head from his book, he spat out these few words to the "ignorant" intruder: "Are you crazy, man? She ain't *white*. She's Irish."

That very confused little white boy stretched himself full length across the desk of the silent Irisher and looked into the darkly brooding face of the Indian. "What all does that mean, Irish?" he asked.

"Well it ain't white, and it ain't Mexican and it sure ain't black. I reckon it's sumpin like Dutch," explained Aisling's hero.

But she wasn't Indian either and she and her sisters needed to embrace their own culture and identity, one that was already complicated enough. They would eventually have to make their way in a world very different from reservation life. The longer we delayed, the harder the transition would be. So, when Geraldine Ann was ready for secondary school, we returned to Ireland. Kaniah Ní Chíosóig, Beautiful Beads, our fourth daughter, was born in Dublin in 1980.

಼

THE POLITICAL SITUATION IN THE NORTH of Ireland was growing more and more unstable every day. Deirdre, Luke, Tommy and I worked together on a nation-wide campaign that demanded the restoration of political status to internees in the North of Ireland. Bobby Sands stood for parliament in the British General Election of 1981, from his prison hospital bed, and won a stunning victory in the constituency of Fermanagh/South Tyrone. Bobby died a few short days later as a result of his sixty-six-day protest fast, and nine young republican prisoners followed him to their graves. Black flags covered the Irish countryside.

It was a time of great political and economic turmoil throughout Ireland. The republican campaigns in the north were slowly beginning to shift gear, moving gradually away from dependence on armed conflict and towards a policy of more active political debate. Former hunger strikers were contesting elections. We were on the picket lines and at the rallies, with Deirdre in tow as often as we could drag her away from Focus. As an avid reader on national and international affairs, she had a wide perspective and strongly held views. At heart, she was a republican, but she agonised constantly over every report of new attacks or ghastly bombing incidents.

Tommy continued moving between London and Dublin, as work opportunities arose and our three older girls progressed steadily through secondary school. I had opened a morning session playschool in Malahide in order to stay at home with our baby Kaniah.

Then, in 1984, our eldest daughter, Geraldine Ann, left Ireland to study geology at the Colorado School of Mines in Golden, Colorado. CSM was the nerve centre for all mineral and energy studies in the United States. The very next year, Aisling received an offer of admission to Cornell University, an Ivy League university situated on the banks of beautiful Lake Cayuga in upstate New York.

Geraldine Ann had left home when she was barely seventeen and had been away for an entire year. She had a will of iron. Since she had begun hunting for fossils with Rita Billie on Big Cypress Reservation, she had known that geology was what she wanted to do. If America was where she could do it, then that's where she'd have to be. And if she had felt lost or lonely over that past year, she had kept it all to herself.

But now Aisling would be leaving for America as well, and neither of them would be coming home for holidays. That, I thought to myself, would be asking too much.

It was, well and truly, "make your mind up" time. There was no way that anyone could keep two girls in college in America, with another one snapping at their heels. Even with scholarships, the cost would be staggering. We would have to take direct action. We sold our house, and everything in it, and headed back to the United States. It was time to learn to fly.

Ⳕ

AISLING HAD ALWAYS BEEN a real home bird. As a baby, she had hated spending a single night out of her own bed. It had taken her longest of all to settle down on the reservation. Now, we were back in America and she and I were heading off on a seven-hour journey aboard a Greyhound Bus to upstate Ithaca, New York, to a college that neither of us had ever seen. I was dropping her off to spend the next four years in a strange country among strangers. This was a long, long way from our small, safe community in County Dublin.

After spending three days with her on a college orientation course, I left again on the Greyhound, and looked back to see tears streaming down Aisling's face. That just about broke my heart. I cried all the way back to New York City and I asked myself, a thousand times over, why was I doing this mad thing?

It all came down to an unending struggle between two places, two identities, two sets of values and divided loyalties. We were back to the Ireland–America tussle once again. Against all the odds, my parents had managed to set five of us on the road to life with good educations. The next generation should do even better. That was the American way.

Unknown to myself, I had absorbed it all. Throughout the many changes and dislocations in our lives, one reality had remained. Our daughters deserved good educations, as good as the one that had been offered to me. Extraordinary opportunities were coming from America. Nothing should deny them their chance.

Breifní, who was fifteen years old at the time, and Kaniah, who was still a child of four, had stayed behind with my cousins in Woodside, Queens, while I travelled to Ithaca with Aisling. The O'Keeffes had never questioned why we had come. The unexpected arrival of relatives from Ireland, followed by some equally sudden departures, was a regular part of Irish-American life.

Now I was back, but I planned to leave almost immediately. The cousins helped us to gather up our suitcases and drove us to New York City's Westside Bus Terminal. We had a daunting thirty-six-hour bus journey to Oklahoma City ahead of us.

We had left Ireland on a balmy, autumn day at the end of August; but August is high summer in America. The heat was excruciating. Sweat poured down our backs and soaked our clothing as we waited in the blazing morning sun to board our bus. And heat was the last thing in the world that Kaniah needed.

Kaniah had begun experiencing serious convulsions from the age of ten months and, after two years of treatment with a bewildering assortment of medications, she had been diagnosed as having an immature brain. Mechanisms that normally filter out an overload of stimuli in young infants had not yet fully developed in Kaniah's brain. Consequently, her brain took in everything.

In order to keep these grand seizures at bay, we had to keep Kaniah's environment quiet and stable. There could be no extremes in her life. Room temperature had to be constant, not too hot and not too cold. We had to keep noise at a minimum. Exposure to flashing or swirling lights was definitely out. Her brain was like an electric socket; if it became overloaded, it would blow. In the fullness of time, it would mature and learn to filter out the overload. Meanwhile, we had to keep her on anti-convulsive medication and carefully monitor her progress.

By the time we were leaving for the United States, the convulsions had stopped but Kaniah was still on medication. We had to ensure that the same conditions prevailed wherever we went, until she was convulsion- and medication-free for at least six months. That was the reason we were heading out west and not south with Tommy, who was hoping to get work on vessels fishing off the Florida Keys. She might not have been able to tolerate the extremely high temperatures and humid conditions of a Floridian summer.

Mercifully, the Greyhound Bus was well air-conditioned and comfortable. We travelled through one industrial city after another, all defined by their towering electricity pylons and their featureless factory complexes. I had been depressed when we started out and I became more and more depressed with every grimy town we passed through. We reached Pittsburgh as dusk was drawing in, and sleep descended upon us. I thanked the Lord for small mercies.

We woke up to a radiant sunrise in the middle of the Ohio Valley, a part of the United States that I had only ever seen in my mind's eye. This was an incredible, amazing, and truly mind-blowing sight: endless fields of gently waving, golden corn. We had entered the breadbasket of America. Never in my wildest dreams could I have imagined such abundance, such magnificence, such plentiful bounty. The proverbial "horn of plenty" swelled and swelled and went on forever.

Breifní and Kaniah were far less impressed. Breifní was convinced that her mother had lost her mind. Her mother had uprooted them from their comfortable home in Ireland, she had shorn them of everything they possessed and she had deposited them on a miserable bus with a dangerous-looking bunch of weirdoes and half a dozen suitcases. She, Breifní, would now have to look after Kaniah because clearly, her mother had completely gone off the rails.

Five bus transfers at five seedy bus stops later, we arrived in the dry, red clay land that is Oklahoma. I was now commencing to agree with the unhappy analysis of my young daughter. I must have taken leave of my senses. It would have to get better than this, real fast.

൫

AND IT DID. Gretta, Patrick and Courtney were waiting to welcome us to their wonderful home in Lake Aluma. Miraculously, Breifní began to relax, now that she was back in the bosom of her family. She commandeered the kitchen and began to display her considerable culinary skills, cooking up a storm of honey-glazed ham and southern fried chicken. Kaniah and Courtney spent their days climbing trees and chasing ducks around the lakeside. Neighbours called, bringing cookies and ice tea for the visitors. Life just ambled quietly along in this tranquil, sun-soaked piece of middle America.

But our lovely respite was to be very short-lived. We were only staying a little while; just long enough to buy a car and, once again, be on our way.

Understandably, Breifní's blood pressure rocketed at the news of our impending departure. Granted, Oklahoma was not Dublin, but at least in Oklahoma we would have had family. Were we now going somewhere that we knew no one at all?

I had considered living in New York but had rejected it as being too dangerous for a woman alone with two children. The West Coast was too far away and too avant-garde. Florida, Oklahoma and Texas were too hot. Colorado was conservative, safe and beautiful. Colorado would be perfect.

Gretta and Patrick helped me to buy a car and insure it and a week after arriving in Oklahoma City, Gretta led us out onto I-40 and pointed us in the direction of Colorado. Drive 540 miles due west and turn right at New Mexico. You are then there.

That long, lonely drive is forever etched in my memory. I talked a blue streak, pointing out every bump in the road and every hazy mountain ridge that came into sight; every crumbling cowboy shack and every lazy oil pump that nodded to us along the way. I half expected to hear the thunder of hooves and see a band of whooping Apaches descending on us from over the far horizon. I had no idea where we were going, apart from the fact that we were heading for Colorado, but I let on that I knew it all, so I wouldn't scare the screaming bejaysus out of my children.

I had taken every precaution that I could. I had bought a brand new car. That should guarantee we would not break down in parts unknown, or have our abandoned carcasses picked clean by encircling buzzards. I had bought a map that I didn't need. The road was as straight as the crow flies. I had stocked up on cold drinks and tasty snacks and I had turned the air-conditioning up to the max. And I prayed — a whole lot!

We were heading across the Texas panhandle, a place known in western legend and song as the badlands. Every single inch of it was true to its name. It was as barren as the surface of the moon. Now and again, like every hundred miles or so, we would pass a senior citizen trundling along the sun-baked road at thirty miles an hour in his recreational vehicle, with a bumper sticker proclaiming "Jesus Saves" or "My Grandbaby is an Honor Student" emblazoned across his rear.

The drive is nothing but a blur in Breifní's mind. She was too traumatised by this apparent flight into madness to absorb any of the awesome landscape that was unfolding before us.

We travelled for nine hours and we stopped only once. That was to use the rest rooms and fill up the petrol tank at a Texaco station in Abilene. As I nervously watched the petrol gauge whizzing past my eyes, a Trailways Bus pulled up beside me. Out stepped a taut and trim Texas Ranger, a serious Stetson hat planted securely on his crew-cut head. He was manacled to a burly, shaven-haired and multi-tattooed prisoner. A dementia of psychedelic patterns paraded across his bald scalp. This remarkable duo were heading for the Texas State Penitentiary, "just a piece down the road". There was no coaxing the children to eat after that. Raw fear had robbed them of their appetites.

We had left the leaden heat of Texas behind and my spirits began to rise as we approached the tri-state area of Texas, New Mexico and Colorado. "Keep your eyes peeled for the Rocky Mountains," I called to Breifní, who was suddenly showing signs of a remarkable resurrection in the back seat. Rising altitude and clear air will do that for you every time.

We were sailing along on the home stretch, passing through the south Colorado town of Pueblo, when the full force of the majestic Rockies came into view. Their snow-covered peaks closed in all around us. I rolled the windows down on my spanking new automobile and the cool, crisp air of a Rocky Mountain high breezed past my face. "Feel that, Breifní? Is that sensational, or what?" I was elated, truly buoyant. We had arrived.

It was getting dark and we had to stop for the night. I was physically, mentally and emotionally exhausted. It's hard work, this business of trying to keep a brave face on things. We could continue in the morning — perhaps travel on to Denver or even Boulder farther north. We would see how the fancy took us after a good night's sleep.

We found a small family-run motel in Colorado Springs and I was able to breathe easy for the first time in several weeks. This felt good. It felt right. I started to believe that this cock-eyed plan was really going to work. We would work, live, seek out opportunities and see our three older daughters through college. Then we could think about the next step.

We arose in the morning to a bright, sunny day, and looked across the road to find that we were facing the Sacred Heart Catholic Church. I was forever asking the good Lord for positive signs to point me along the way, and I took this one to be a real whopper!

It was Labour Day weekend, the last of the summer holidays on the American calendar. I bought a local newspaper and retreated to my motel room to peruse the home rental ads. And I discovered a notable feature in quite a few of them. The more prominent ads highlighted the fact that they were situated in the Cheyenne Mountain School District. "That has to be the best neighbourhood to live in," I reasoned to Breifní and Kaniah, and anyone else who cared to listen. "Wherever it is, that's where we should be."

It was Sunday on a big holiday weekend, but this being America, some real estate offices were open and ready for business. I telephoned an apartment complex called Broadmoor Villas and made an immediate appointment to view. The new school year would begin on the following Tuesday. That gave me two days to find an apartment, and an address, and enrol my girls in school.

The motel in which we were staying was but a short drive away. We crossed a stunning mountain pass lined with lush forests of maple and beech, and the crimson and gold of their early autumn leaves took my breath away. Even Breifní was getting excited. Things were looking good. The narrow mountain pass opened out onto a broad tree-lined avenue that led up to the glistening waters of clear blue lake. This was Broadmoor. This was God's own country. And this is where we would live for the next three years.

ೞ

WE NOW HAD AN APARTMENT and an address. Breifní became a student at Cheyenne Mountain High School and Kaniah began kindergarten at Pauline Memorial Catholic School. They were safe and secure in good schools, in the best of neighbourhoods. I would have no drugs and no gang wars to worry about here. Now I needed to find a job.

Fitting that part of the jigsaw together was not quite so easy. Colorado State teachers need accreditation from the State Department of Education, whether they work in public, private or parochial schools. Applicants need to fulfil all the relevant college course specifications and pass the Colorado Teacher's Licence Exam in three areas: American History, English and Mathematics. It would take me at least six months to file my papers and prepare for the exam, then another six months to sit the exam and wait for the results. That would mean the best part of a year — completely shot! Sitting around idle for a year was not an option. I had to pay the rent. So I did what a lot of mothers with school-age children do. I joined Merry Maids.

I was up at 6.00 am every morning. I organised the girls for school, scraped the ice off the car, dropped the girls off at school, and then drove though blinding snow blizzards to the offices of Merry Maids. My work partner was a Mexican girl named Maritza. She also had two school-age children and we both had to be finished by 2.30 in order to collect our children from school. So, the arrangement suited me to perfection.

The pay was good and the hours were just what I needed. But the work was hellishly hard. We cleaned houses and were paid according to the number and size of the houses we completed. The faster and more efficiently we worked, the more money we earned. We recorded every task that we completed on a company checklist. Then the senior partner — that was Maritza — left a signed copy of the list for the customer and turned the original in at the office. Americans are not slow at complaining, so there was never a chance of cutting corners or slackening off in the pursuit of ready cash.

This was a thoroughly professional operation. The main city roads were always cleared of snow and ice by early morning, so Maritza and I were able to zip around the Springs in our canary yellow aprons and armed with compact tool kits filled with vacuum cleaners, disinfectants, leather chamoises, and Murphy's beeswax furniture polish. Merry Maids did not do windows.

We were good. We were *really* good. We were *so* good that Maritza wanted us to open a franchise of our own. But I had other things on my mind. By the end of our first year in Colorado Springs, I had passed the state licensing exam and was teaching eighth-grade history and English at Kaniah's school, Pauline Memorial.

Geraldine Ann and Aisling were now coming home for their summer breaks and they had secured exciting holiday work with the national state parks. Aisling was an interpreter for visitors to the Garden of the Gods National Park and Geraldine Ann was team leader of an environmental programme for teenagers in the Colorado Springs City Parks. But in time, Breifní landed the plummiest job of all. She got to mix gallons of Brazilian cocoa, fresh cream, rice crispies, golden nuts and plump sweet raisins in huge copper vats and produce the rich and succulent, the absolutely sinful Rocky Mountain Chocolates.

The magnificent Rocky Mountains with their constantly changing colours and their crystalline lakes, their glorious golden summers and their snow-white winters could capture a heart of stone. Tommy was working in Florida, but he was able to visit for long intervals on a regular basis. We would have been happy to remain in Colorado forever.

The friendships we had made on Big Cypress had remained strong down through the years and I had received repeated invitations from my old colleagues to return to Big Cypress. The bilingual programme that we had established in 1978 was flagging and it was in dire need of resuscitation. Now that Kaniah had passed the danger zone, having been convulsion- and medication-free for two years, I could consider returning to the Seminoles.

We loved Colorado and our way of life there. We did not want to leave. But the Seminoles had given us much more than we had given them. They had welcomed us and been our trusted and loyal friends. I owed them. I had no good reason to refuse.

We left Colorado in 1988 with very heavy hearts. Colorado, too, had been good to us. We would miss it.

ᚲᛞ

I WENT BACK TO WORK with the Seminoles and this time I had Kaniah with me. Unsurprisingly, there was another Kaniah in her third-grade class, Kaniah Jim, and quite surprisingly, there was a little Seminole girl named Breifní. It was, I thought, a fair exchange.

We spent two more happy and fruitful years on Big Cypress. The Miccosukee programme was back on track. However, by that time, Breifní had entered Texas A&M University. Now, we had three girls attending colleges in three different parts of a very big United States. Tommy and I were living in a fourth part of it. It was not at all clear how we were going to manage it all.

I began poring through education periodicals, searching for anything that would shed some light on our challenging situation. A chance reply to an unusual advertisement in the *Educator's Monthly* magazine brought me an unexpected but positive response.

A newly established copper mine, located in the Atacama Desert of Chile, was looking for a professional educator to set up a school facility for dependent children of expatriate workers in the city of Antofagasta. The successful applicant would then have to manage the facility and teach in it. I was a teacher with a curriculum development background. I had no business experience. I had never done anything as extensive as this project envisioned. Nonetheless, after a series of interviews and an on-site visit, management offered me the job.

That, I argued to myself, had to mean that I was able to do it. I accepted, with my heart in my mouth and a prayer in my heart. I decided that, come what may, I would remain in Chile until the three girls had finished college. Then we would all go home to Dublin.

Kaniah attended the local primary school in Antofagasta, and switched from the Miccosukee language to Spanish for the next four years. We did return to Ireland after Breifní had graduated from Texas A&M and, after another brief spell in Dublin, Kaniah and I went to live in northern Tanzania. I was once again engaged in curriculum development; this time as part of an Ireland Aid programme that was designed to help primary school teachers to teach in schools that had no books and no equipment. That was no mean task.

Kiswahili became the language of instruction for Kaniah at the local Shule Mazoezi in Korogwe. It sounds almost as though she would have had to be as old as Methuselah by that time, but no, she returned to do the last three years of secondary school at Coláiste Mhuire, in Parnell Square, where the language of instruction was Irish. She survived it all, slightly battered and a little bruised but still on her feet. She is now studying Spanish and Portuguese at Queen's University in Belfast.

And our experiences in all those places? Well, *sin scéal eile*. That's another story, to be told at another time.

ଔ

Chapter 9

REQUIEM FOR DEIRDRE

D EIRDRE O'CONNELL'S DYNAMIC LITTLE STUDIO and theatre
was gaining critical acclaim against all the odds. In 1968, the
Irish Times arts critic wrote, "Dublin Focus Theatre is performing a
great service to this city and country by its integrity, dedication
and the excellence of its actors." In 1969, *The Irish Times* again
wrote: "Like everything we have seen at the Focus, these pieces
are played with scrupulous attention to detail and they acquire
that authority which springs from discipline." The *Evening Press*
said: "This is the only theatre in the country which regularly puts
on great plays. And I mean the only theatre. It is also unique and
exciting in its methods of approaching a play. Definitely hard-
made stuff."

Yet against this background of resounding tributes, Focus was
constantly on the precipice of closure. A 73-seat capacity would
never make money, no matter how many full houses they could
fill over any given period of time. And they could not transfer
successful productions to larger houses because they could not
pay equity rates on a full-time basis.

In the early years of Focus's life, several situations arose which
illustrate vividly the trap in which they were firmly locked. Following exceptionally successful runs of *Uncle Vanya* in 1969 and *A
Doll's House* in 1972, the Peacock Theatre invited the Focus company to transfer. Both times, the invitation was withdrawn at the
request of Irish Actors' Equity. Focus could not pay equity rates

and was therefore not eligible for Equity management status. Consequently, Equity houses such as the Peacock could not be made available to them. This became the uncompromising policy of the actors' union for many years to come.

How utterly ironic! The cause to which our Dad had dedicated his life — the building of the labour union movement — was now becoming the undoing of Deirdre's dream.

Drama critics and the public alike were very aware of the invaluable service Focus delivered to Irish theatre. In 1974, the *Evening Press* wrote:

> Considering its size and resources, the Focus Theatre probably offers better value for money than any other theatrical establishment in Dublin. It operates on a shoe-string and could not survive without the assistance of the Friends of Focus, of whom there are now 128; yet it manages to come up regularly with the type of quality and meaty plays one would not see anywhere else.

They were firmly caught in the poverty trap and would need an innovative plan to move forward.

Under the able direction of Mary Elizabeth and Declan Burke-Kennedy, Focus set about fundraising in earnest. Focus Week became a regular feature every year, presenting the best of Irish literary arts. Seamus Heaney, Benedict Kiely, Anthony Cronin and Niall Toibin presented their works in the tiny venue; from the jazz world came Louis Stewart, Jim Doherty and the Noel Kelehan Quintet; folk nights presented people like Luke Kelly, Frank Harte, Mick Fitzgerald, Liam Weldon and Al O'Donnell; and they even managed cabaret with the likes of Ann Bushnell, Fran Dempsey, Danny Doyle and Colm Wilkinson. The Friends of Focus continued to assist with annual subscriptions and loyal words of encouragement, and subventions from the Arts Council and Dublin Corporation increased marginally with the passing years.

Deirdre's fine on-stage performances were consistently applauded with expressions such as, "powerful, splendidly controlled, committed, subtle technique, a masterful characterisation" and "a tour de force" being repeated again and again.

Focus Theatre and its dedicated company were not just critically acclaimed. Ireland's plain people were often moved to pen their appreciation, not for publication but out of pure joy. T. Monaghan, from Cootehill, County Cavan said this in a letter to Deirdre:

> I left the Focus as I have left the Théatre Nationale Populaire in Paris, with a sense of elation and an awareness that theatre is alive. I had become involved in the thoughts and feelings of others. There was a starkness about the acting that made me mistake it for life. The effect was increased by the one round of applause at the end of each act. At Focus, there is no limelighting.

End of production "bops" at their home in "The Dart" became the thing of legend. With a table laden with chunks of cheese and brown bread and copious bottles of red wine, Deirdre would hitch up layers of black skirt and let rip, bopping and weaving on her spindly black-encased legs to the music of John Lennon, the Beatles, Frank and Dino and, in latter days, Travis. It was a rare and quare sight to behold, the disciplined and controlled Deirdre O'Connell rocking 'til dawn.

cg

DEIRDRE'S LIFE INTERESTS extended far beyond the theatre world and she remained committed to issues of social justice throughout her life. She worked closely with Dr Kadar Asmal, former Law Lecturer at Trinity College and now Minister of Education in the Republic of South Africa, raising the profile of the Irish Anti-Apartheid Movement in the 1980s. It was through her intercession that such artistes as Luke Kelly and Mary Black performed for the H-Block/Armagh Hunger Strike Campaign at a time when such manifestations were not considered to be politically correct. One of her most prized possessions was a Bobby Sands memorial plaque, presented to her by the H-Block Committee in recognition of her unwavering support. It hung above her fireplace beside a bronze statue of the stricken Celtic warrior, Cuchulainn, strapped as he was to a boulder so he would die on his feet. Luke had given the statue to our Dad and it too became Deirdre's inheritance.

Deirdre and Luke were becoming major forces on the Irish music and theatre scenes and their lives together resonated with all the tension, vibrancy and struggle that such compelling personalities bring. On one rare occasion when Deirdre reminisced about her life with Luke, she recalled, "We were very simple in our ways, both working class people and proud of it." Their marriage was not always an easy or conventional one, surrounded as they were by legions of fans and onlookers and Luke's unyielding socialist principles. "Luke was a committed socialist who lived his principles to the full," continued Deirdre. "He actually kept people — for years and years. Because he was what he said he was. I didn't always find it comfortable, mind you — waking up with somebody at the bottom of my bed! Or trying to get into my own loo and finding somebody sleeping in the bathtub!"

Deirdre needed her private space and the constant presence of "friends", who were often strangers, in their home began to sow seeds of discord. Luke was, in Deirdre's words, an "internal" person. He could drift down the stairs of Dartmouth Square, newspaper stuffed under his arm and cap jammed on top of his unruly mop, and continue on out the front door without seeing a living soul. Deirdre couldn't. She wanted that private space.

As a young man in his twenties, Luke had been a solidly built and clean-shaven youth with a craggy face and spectacular smile. But with the growing success of The Dubliners both at home and abroad, the harsh demands of a touring life began to show. Physically, Luke grew thinner while his mass of unruly red hair was accompanied by a red scraggy beard.

In 1976, The Dubliners successfully toured New Zealand, Australia, Germany, Holland, Scandinavia, Belgium and France and they continued to play to packed houses at the Royal Albert Hall and most major concert halls throughout Britain. In 1977, impresario and producer Noel Pearson offered Luke the role of Pontius Pilate in the stage production of *Jesus Christ Superstar*.

Deirdre was less than thrilled. While she believed implicitly in Luke's talent and powerful stage presence, she was not convinced that this was the way he should go. But when his much applauded success was followed by an appearance in the adaptation of Brendan Behan's *Richard's Cork Leg* in Dublin and London, Luke's career seemed about to take an unexpected turn to the musical stage.

The Dubliners returned to sold-out concerts in New Zealand and Australia in 1979 and again 1980. By this time, Luke's health was in serious decline. Because he was experiencing excruciating headaches and frequent and severe dizzy spells, he was eventually hospitalised back home in Ireland. Major surgery discovered the existence of a large but operable brain tumour.

Luke recovered somewhat and returned to the stage, thrilling his audiences once again with his unique and powerful performances. But in 1984, at the age of forty-three, Luke suffered a massive brain haemorrhage and tragically died. Years of touring the world with The Dubliners had exacted a heavy toll; the tumour had taken his life.

ⓒ

DEIRDRE WAS INCONSOLABLE. But her fierce pride and independent streak stood in the way of intervention, both personally and professionally. Luke's passing left a void in her life that only Focus could fill. She was on stage the following week, "which is the way Luke would have it".

She worked to the point of exhaustion; teaching, acting, directing and running the theatre. During the decade that stretched from 1980 through 1990, Focus produced over forty plays, not including lunchtime performances. The breadth of the work was staggering. It included plays by Ibsen, Lorca, Arthur Miller, Brian Friel, Tennessee Williams, Strindberg, Athol Fugard, Marsha Norman, Samuel Beckett, Edward Albee, Charles Dickens, Eduardo Manet, D.H. Lawrence, Doris Lessing, Nikolai Gogol, Willie Russell, Luigi Pirandello, Lyle Kessler, and Clifford Odets. The seasons of new Irish writers included works by Declan Burke-Kennedy, Robert Emmet Meagher, Mary Elizabeth Burke-Kennedy, Tony Cafferty, William Trevor, Ena May, Tom O'Neill and Peter Tenson. Deirdre continued to conduct her classes in the Stanislavsky Studio every Saturday of her life, because Studio was at the core of her Focus vision.

In a splendid analysis of the Stanislavsky system for *Magill* magazine in September 1984, Nick Carter concluded his article with this: "The basis of Focus is sheer hard work — informed and informing — which issues forth in acting that involves the audience less in the traditional suspension of disbelief than in simple belief itself. No other theatre in the city can boast of such a tradition."

During the thirty years of teaching the Stanislavsky system, the fees Deirdre collected never rose above three pounds for a five- or six-hour session. She never handled money herself. The student fees were dropped into a cardboard box inside the front door and Deirdre seldom knew who had paid and who had not. Her needs and her pleasures were simple. At the close of each session, she would turn off the lights, lock the theatre door and follow her actors down to Hourican's Pub for a glass of red wine and a chat.

Deirdre was blessed throughout her life with a loyal band of true friends. They were ever-present in times of need but they also understood and respected her desires for a private life. O'Brien's of Leeson Street was the retreat she sought when she wanted to think, to plan, to learn her lines, or just to be on her own.

She never took holidays and Sunday was her only day of rest. Occasionally, she would relent and accept an invitation to either the Cusacks', the O'Connells' or the Kellys'. Deirdre would not hear of being picked up and transported to our house by car. She would dash across the city from the south side of the Liffey to Talbot Street with her quick little steps, her countless black shawls flying around her head and that venerable clipboard held firmly under her arm. At the bus stop outside Guiney's Clothing Store, she would catch the number 42 heading our way. She always sat downstairs, because she had never outgrown the dreaded travel sickness. The upstairs level was just too bumpy.

But we could never be sure what time Deirdre would arrive, considering the number of urgent phone calls she would have to make, or the playbills she would have to hang, or the people she would first need to meet. Then there would be a final stop at Amnesty International, to gather up a grab-bag full of little trinkets for our girls and their friends.

She would arrive in great form, spinning intriguing yarns filled with pungent pauses, and then restarting the tale mid-sentence, leaving the listener to fill in the gaps. Eventually, after a quick cup of strong coffee or a glass of red wine, the children would prevail upon her to go out into the garage where they kept a tea chest filled with a wild collection of old shoes, handbags and bundles of dress-up clothes. The neighbours' children would know that Deirdre had come. They would have seen and heard her skipping along the green, hand-in-hand with our three girls, singing "Skip to My Lou" at the top of their voices.

The pals would appear at our door as though on cue. Out there in the garage, Deirdre would take them through a mad series of improvisations, dependent totally on the crazy assortment of costumes that the children had managed to throw on. It often reminded me of the hair-brained antics we had got up to as children back on East 139th Street.

Deirdre would revel in the food, the drink and the *craic* but she would insist on being back in Focus that night. It was as though she needed its very air to breathe.

Deirdre had never been a great sleeper but sleep deprivation now became a chronic source of misery. Nonetheless, it was during this period of inner turmoil that she produced some of her finest work. In 1984, in a review of *Night Mother* by Marsha Norman, Con Houlihan wrote, "The acting of Ena May and Deirdre O'Connell is superb. I would have called it stunning only that I wasn't surprised . . . in direction and design, you have theatre at its finest."

In 1985, *Hello and Goodby*, by South African playwright Athol Fugard, opened in the middle of the Dublin Theatre Festival, quite independently and without fanfare of any kind. According to renowned author and theatre critic Colm Toibin:

> The fact that Deirdre O'Connell has acted for so long in the same place has diverted attention away from what a wonderful actor she is . . . how again and again she approaches a part with skill and understanding, how she fills up the stage with a nervous predatory air, using her shoulders and arms, the angle of her head, the rise and fall of her voice to move from utter menace to intense desolation. (*Sunday Independent*, 13 October 1985).

In that same year, she was presented with Harvey's Theatre Award for Outstanding Contributions to Irish Theatre.

Letters and telegrams of congratulations flowed in from actors, directors, critics and the general public. But the words of appreciation from former students touched her most. She kept every card, letter and photograph ever sent to her. Her home was an obstacle course. You had to navigate your way among stacks of scripts and books, and letters, postcards, trinkets and remembrances from family, well-wishers and friends in order to gain entry.

Deirdre directed the award-winning performance of Tim McDonnell in *Diary of a Madman* by Nicolai Gogol in 1987 and in 1991, Brian Di Salvo's direction of Arthur Miller's, *A View from the Bridge* was widely acknowledged as the home triumph of the Dublin Theatre Festival. It played to packed houses and, by popular demand and with the relaxation of Equity's policies on management and membership, this highly successful production transferred to the Andrew's Lane Theatre.

By this time, the Stanislavsky Studio had trained a new generation for the Focus Theatre Company. Ger Carey, Brent Hearne, Paul Roe, Elizabeth Moynihan, Stephanie Dunne, Mary Ryan, Paul Keeley, Luke Hayden, Jayne Snow, Liam Halligan, Mary Moynihan, Paul Bennett, Ken Harmon, Paul Raynor, Eamon Hunt, Guy Carlton, Donal O'Kelly, Sean Campion, Phyl Doherty, Michael Campion, Savio Sequiera, Jarlath Fahy, Ann Maloney-O'Driscoll, Ann Russell-Wheatley, Olwen Fouere, Tristan Gribben, Bairbre Ní Caoimhe, Michelle Costelloe, Michelle Manahan, Colin Rothery, Tom Laidlaw, Joan Sheehy, Alan Gilsenan, Kevin O'Brien, Kevin Sheridan, Mariosa de Faoite, Carmel White, Robbie McDowell, Hazel Dunphy, Jackie Nugent, Carmel Nugent, Síle Nugent, Niamh Mahon, Maeve Leonard, Paul Lawrence, Aisling McLoughlin, Aoibhinn Gilroy, Lisa Curran, Margaret Twomey, Orlaigh de Burca, Robert Lane, Ronan Wilmot, Robbie Doolin, Ena May, Rebecca Schull, Malachy McKenna, Ciaran Walsh, Joe Campbell, Áine Ní Murchú, Mary Wilson, Helene Brown, Lucy Bradell, Geraldine Maguire, Tony McCormick, Dan Kole, Áine Cusack, Liz Cosgrove, David Johnston and Eileen Fennell are only some of the scores of accomplished actors and directors who studied and worked with Deirdre for over thirty-five years.

In studio or on stage, Deirdre was chillingly perceptive. But, according to her lifetime friend and close associate, Sabina Coyne-Higgins, she had a special gift that enabled her to ask just the right probing questions, ones that would help actors reveal for themselves the truths that they needed to uncover. She would encourage them to explore endless possibilities and access every available source, sources that might be hidden within their own experiences. Ultimately, this exploration would lead them to a deeper understanding of the characters they were to become.

Tim McDonnell, who will shortly direct the current Stanislavsky Studio, has said: "Deirdre encouraged us to have an imaginatively real response to a situation, involving organic dramatic subtlety rather than a mechanical piece of clichéd play-acting. We were being exposed to the sort of exercise that even now would be considered advanced." (*Irish Times* Weekend Arts by Katie Donovan, 1992). In the words of Tom Hickey, Deirdre was always "more of guide than a dogmatic teacher".

But Ger Carey, who joined the Studio in 1988, expressed regret at what he saw as neglect by the Arts Council of Deirdre's achievements. In the same interview, Ger said, "She [Deirdre] should be spared the worry of the rent for the theatre building, or worrying about whether the roof leaks. She charges a ridiculously low amount for the weekend Studio sessions and she's embarrassed to take the money. She has shown her commitment to the theatre and this should be acknowledged."

Everything that related to Focus concerned her, from acting and directing to the condition of the roof and the state of the loo. No one who hasn't experienced first-hand the sheer volume of work and spiritual dedication that she poured into keeping that show on the road could possibly believe the extent of it. You would hear her before you could see her, as her quick steps hurried along Pembroke Lane to the theatre, her throaty voice demanding to know why nobody had done anything yet about the cigarette butts that littered the path from the performance the night before.

In 1988, Gabriel Byrne, one of Deirdre's celebrated theatre veterans, had this to say:

> Dressed in her customary suit of solemn black, this flame-haired female Hamlet seduced me into a world of Ibsen and Chekhov, Lorca and Strindberg, with her passion and commitment and unconditional love of the theatre. You will see plays here, in Focus, that you will see nowhere else in Ireland. With miniscule grants, this unsinkable woman has

given the country some of its finest productions and a fair percentage of its best actors. As Dublin is a place where you keep meeting people you know, no matter how short a time you've been here, you may possibly see her blurring past you to hang posters or cajole money from the Arts Council or do whatever the thousand and one things are that she does to keep her tiny ship afloat. And if you do call out to her, as everyone in Dublin does, "Howya Deirdre", she's bound to know your name.

Although Deirdre's public persona was a familiar one to Irish theatre lovers and theatre goers for all those years, her private life was always her own. She continued to guard it with the same determination she had shown in guiding her vision for Focus.

In an interview with Siobhan Crozier in 1990, Deirdre said that she regarded Luke as her life partner and dismissed any conjecture about their social arrangements as banal and trivial. Though they lived apart during the final years of Luke's life, they were still constant companions around town.

"I adore him now as much as I ever adored him," said Deirdre. "Luke is so unique. Luke is so extraordinary, he was a deeply, profoundly human man — the best person I have ever known or ever will."

"She doesn't give a damn that people might think her unhinged when she says that she talks to him every day," continued the interview:

"I have had this huge, immensely beautiful experience of Luke and that's pretty good. Some people call me cracked but if I ask Luke to give me a leg-up, he does! I don't know what that means but I believe it."

She acknowledges that she often needs that leg-up, battling on for her tiny theatre. Its influence and significance has permeated around the world, with many of the most talented Irish actors coming back from Hollywood and beyond to remember the debt they owe to Focus. As an excellent cast fight it out in *Virginia Woolf* every night, they're bedevilled by their lack of funds to keep their theatre alive, none more so than Deirdre O'Connell, Doc to her company, who won't give up, won't give in, but swears blind that she can't go on.

With the passing of time, when talking about the audacity she had displayed in launching her dream, Deirdre had become more philosophical. "Perhaps I might have been overwhelmed or over-awed by such a project if it had not been for my education," said Deirdre, when asked to explain the vision she held at the age of twenty-three.

> "One of the beauties of theatre is that it provides different ways of learning to see oneself. I have always been sublimely unselfconscious, which seems to go against the popular view of theatre people, that they tend to be self-absorbed and self-analytical. Perhaps it might have been better for Focus if I had considered the politics of the feminist question. I think I was treated as a precocious and gifted but not very sensible young woman."

And she continues:

> "What has pleased me most is the extent to which we have remained as much a company as we have. There is still a permanency, still a nucleus of people. We have never had to become freelance emigrants in spite of all the poverty; we have that kind of loyalty, dedication to a common ideal. What has saddened me most is that they all couldn't afford to do so because I have not had enough money to pay them.

> "I would love to do a full season with all the wealth of Focus back in company. Many can only afford to come back once a year. To have them all back together for a season — the talent would blind you." (From "Dublin Women in the Arts".)

Given Deirdre O'Connell's striking appearance, her consistently brilliant stage performances, her life-long commitment to the Stanislavsky Studio and Focus Theatre and her life with Luke Kelly, it is hardly surprising that her work and her life provoked media speculation from time to time. There was only one occasion on which she was known to publicly respond. It was to an article written about her in the *Sunday Tribune* in 1991. Her response was typical of the woman she was.

Dear Sir:

May I reply to your column, "Ulysses" by Fiona Looney of 10 March 1991. During my 23¼ years of work with Focus Theatre the odd, strange comment has been written about me in the press. As it happens, I have never publicly reacted. I am inclined to believe that self-praise is no praise, self-defence no defence, but Fiona Looney really beats the band and I feel I must respond with a note of discord.

I myself directed the Focus stage production of Diary of a Madman, which played in the Project Arts Centre and the Peacock Theatre, Dublin, winning for Tim McDonnell the "Harvey Theatre Award" for best actor in 1987 and which also played in Landon and New York. In New York, Tim won the prestigious "OBIE Award" for Outstanding Performance by an actor. In 1988, Ronan O'Leary directed the film version of Diary of a Madman, based on the Focus production. Given Ronan's film knowledge and flare, I hope and believe it will be a wonderful success.

I played a very small role in Ronan's film. I have not been "tempted out of the theatre". I responded to a strongly felt request to contribute to the film. I agreed with pleasure, as I admired Ronan's approach in the material and my dear friend and colleague Tim McDonnell's performance so much; nothing more, nothing less.

I wish to correct Fiona's statement that I have not been in a play "anywhere else" than Focus. I have played in several theatres in New York, on and off Broadway, including The Ambassador, The Sheridan Street Playhouse, The Actors Play House and Carnegie Hall when it comprised a theatre directed by Saul Colin.

In Ireland I have played at the Pike Theatre, Dublin, The Group Theatre and Everyman Theatre, Cork, The New Ross Theatre and Gorey Arts Theatre, Wexford, City Theatre and Belltable Arts Centre, Limerick, Hawks Well, Sligo, The Jesuit

Hall, Galway, Kilkenny Arts Theatre, Kilkenny and the Little Theatre, Athlone.

The fact that I have worked, in Ireland, exclusively *with* Focus, not *in* Focus, since 1967 is simply because I believe in quality and commitment. I am happy that it has been a great pleasure, not a deprivation. As for being a recluse, I am to be found in full view (when I am not directing or training actors), on stage, mainly in Focus,

> Deirdre O'Connell
> Artistic Director
> The Focus Theatre
> 6 Pembroke Place
> Dublin 2

CB

ON THE 23RD OF NOVEMBER 1997, Focus Theatre celebrated "Thirty Years of Magic". On that joyous occasion, with the Focus Family on stage and spilling out onto Pembroke Lane, Ireland's former Minister for Arts and Culture, Michael D. Higgins declared Deirdre O'Connell, "The greatest single influence in Irish Theatre since the 1960s."

A plaque that sets out an astonishing anthology of more than 150 full-scale productions, not including at least another 100 lunchtime productions, now hangs in the tiny coffee room at the back of the theatre. In the *Cork Examiner*, Patricia Danaher described it as

> a little salon where you pour your own wine from the large bottles of Valpolicella left out, or wait until someone makes you a mug of tea from the ornate silver boiler behind the counter. . . . The *grande dame* of Focus Theatre is Deirdre O'Connell, an actress and teacher. As she floats about the theatre or the salon at the back, you almost feel like a treasured guest in her home. On the wall of the salon, among the many photos and posters of past productions is a photo of the very young and mischievous looking Dubliners, which has to be seen for the way they might look at you. Beside this

photo is an astonishing watercolour of Luke Kelly playing and in mid-song. The colours are so shockingly brilliant, that he looks alive and ablaze. The Focus is a place with a heart and a soul, a lot of history and the warm presence of Deirdre O'Connell, who greets you, sees you off and checks to make sure you're warm. The rest you will have to do yourself.

In the *Sunday Independent* of 4 January 1998, Ciara Dwyer put it like this:

As you speak to Deirdre, she doesn't so much answer as perform. Her casual conversation is dramatic — full of pauses, sweeping hand gestures and that beautifully resonant voice. Her turquoise eyes seem miles away. We are still in the middle of a dramatic pause. If ever there was a female Michael MacLiammoir, Deirdre is it.

During the millennium year and into the early part of 2001, film producers Ronan O'Leary and Ann McRory undertook a daunting project: to document the life work of Deirdre O'Connell. The completed feature-length documentary, *Hold the Passion*, stars Deirdre and features Gabriel Byrne, Sean Campion, Tom Hickey and the cast of Focus Theatre. It is a beautifully crafted and fitting tribute to a remarkable woman; an artist, an actor, a teacher, a visionary, a daughter, a wife, a sister and a friend.

In October of the year 2000, the newly formed fifty-five-piece Dublin City Chamber Orchestra made its first recording; the score for *Hold the Passion*, composed by C.S.L. Parker, and launched it at the National Concert Hall on the 21st of April 2001. Among the packed house were Deirdre's brothers and sisters who had come home to celebrate the wonder that was her life's work. But it was more than that. It was a celebration of the rocky mountain lands of Banteer and Ballisodare and the concrete streets of the South Bronx. It was a celebration of faith and fun, of the endurance, tenacity and true grit of all those who had gone before.

ങ

DEIRDRE O'CONNELL DIED suddenly on the 10th of June, 2001.

ભ

IRISH THEATRE CRITIC AND JOURNALIST, Con Houlihan, was a long-time admirer of Deirdre and her work. There is no more fitting tribute to her than the words he wrote in the programme for Tom Hickey's presentation of *The Gallant John-Joe*, performed in Focus a fortnight after Deirdre departed this life. It captures the essence of Deirdre, from her childhood in the South Bronx to the converted garage in Pembroke Lane:

> Deirdre O'Connell reminded me of Johnny Appleseed, the legendary American who travelled throughout the New World encouraging people to plant orchards. He did so not for fame and least of all for fortune but from love of the noble fruit. Deirdre was lucky in the place and in the time of her girlhood. Franklin Roosevelt had led the country out of The Great Depression; the War had been won. The President was no more but he had left behind a country where people could hope and dream. Deirdre was born in New York in 1939. She grew up a child of a buoyant America.
>
> Her father was a native of Sligo. Her mother came from Cork. They were enlightened parents and encouraged her ambition to give all to Hecuba. She prepared for her hazardous profession in the famous Actors' Studio presided over by Lee Strasberg. There she imbibed the philosophy of Constantin Stanislavsky, the Founder of The Moscow Art Theatre. This doctrine became the seedbed of her career.
>
> On a visit to Ireland in her student days she came to know that great woman of the theatre, Ursula White-Lennon. With her help and advice she decided to settle in Dublin. She came back when she was 23. The big adventure of her life was about to begin. Her driving desire was to have a theatre of her own. The quest became the stuff of black comedy as oasis after oasis turned out to be a mirage. Eventually she found a disused factory in a half-hidden part of Dublin. Two dear friends of mine, her husband Luke Kelly and Mick McCarthy of the

Embankment, helped to transform this unlikely setting into a house of dreams. Thus, The Focus came into being. Never was a theatre better christened — the word means "fireplace" in Latin. It could hold only about four score but this drawback gave it a rare intimacy.

There a generation of players were educated — and aficionados of the theatre experienced works that otherwise they might not have been seen. Familiar plays were not ignored but the great virtue of The Focus was the production of lesser-known plays by famous authors, especially those of Ibsen and Strindberg and Sartre and Miller. For good measure, there were plays by not-so-famous dramatists from mainland Europe and The United States. Deirdre showed her boldness in adapting works by Herman Hesse and Doris Lessing and Marguerite Duras.

Deirdre's beauty and talent could have ferried her to world fame but she kept her eyes fixed on her lonely star. Noel Pearson offered her very attractive money to play in *One Flew Over The Cuckoo's Nest*; the part might have been written for her but it was an invitation she could refuse.

When he told me, I was reminded of a story in Walter Starkie's autobiography. While collecting music in Spain, he visited a famous singer in the high country of Castille. He sang for him but only on condition that he wasn't recorded. He said: "If you take my songs to Madrid, they will not be mine anymore." It was a kind of mystical attitude but Starkie understood.

Deirdre's heroic commitment to her art reminded me of a story about Edward Thomas, the English poet who lost his life in the First World War. He too was single-minded. The love he bore to poetry was at fault. His life was a constant struggle against penury; he was so independent that he wouldn't take a regular job. Eventually a friend said to him, "Edward, there is a brilliant young psychiatrist who has just set up practice in London. Go to him and you will be a new man." "Yes," said the poet, "but then I won't be Edward Thomas any more."

Deirdre uttered her own epitaph. "I will never change — and there is no point in trying to change me." Seldom did one person give so much to so many.

Like Johnny Appleseed, she will never die. God rest her fine mind and her brave heart and her noble soul.

CB

AT DEIRDRE'S REQUIEM MASS, from the Church where she and Luke had been married, Breifní Cusack put into words what so many of us were feeling:

My name is Breifní and I am Deirdre's godchild and niece. On a day which is shrouded in profound sorrow and emptiness from the loss of Deirdre, so dearly loved, from all our lives, I would like to share with you a glimpse of life as a child with as magical a person as Deirdre O'Connell, your wild and willowy aunt. It might bring you an unexpected smile.

When my sisters and I were children, we lived in a far, far away little coastal town called Malahide, an enormous thirty-minutes bus ride from our aunt's bustling stomping grounds in the big city. Every two weeks or so, our aunt would pack up her scripts and shawls and her multitude of bags and make her epic half-hour journey on the Number 42 out to the countryside. My sisters and I would walk down to the village bus stop and perch ourselves on the bench and wait for her arrival.

Exactly which Number 42 she would arrive on was anyone's guess because as we are all, I'm sure, all too familiar, punctual to Deirdre would be to arrive on or around the actual day as arranged, sometime between dawn and dusk. And so we would wait and wait, swinging our legs until we spotted that regal crown of red through the window. When she disembarked the 42, we would link arms and set off on the mile home, three-quarters of which was skipped at full toe-tripping speed, and during which we would sing at full voice a song, which she had taught us as babies. I can think of no more appropriate words to recite at this moment:

Zippidy doo dah, Zippidy ay
My, oh my, what a wonderful day
Plenty of sunshine heading my way
Zippidy doo dah, zippidy ay.
There's a bluebird on my shoulder
It's the truth, it's actual
Everything is satisfactual
Zippidy doo dah, Zippidy ay
Wonderful feeling, wonderful day.

We know that she will forever fly like a bluebird.

ൟ

THE FOCUS THEATRE BOARD has been re-formed, with Joe Devlin as artistic director, a committed band of in-house volunteers and a rapidly growing family of Friends of Focus co-ordinated by Breifní O'Connell Cusack. The Stanislavsky Studio will forge ahead, with Timothy O'Donnell heading a panel of Stanislavsky-trained teachers including Ann Maloney O'Driscoll, Liam Halligan, Paul Keeley, Bairbre Ní Caoimhe and Ena May. A three-year plan has been developed and presented to the Arts Council and Deirdre's dream for a full season with "the wealth of Focus back in company" may indeed come to pass.

ൟ

THERE IS A STRANGE LITTLE POSTSCRIPT to the saga of Deirdre and Luke.

Two weeks after Deirdre's burial, I set off on a Sunday morning, intent on paying her a visit and tidying away the mountain of flowers that had been piled high on the sod. I couldn't bear the thought of flowers withering away on her grave. So I drove out to Glasnevin and, noticing that the cemetery gates were open, I drove in.

I had been to that particular graveside many times before, on the occasions of Luke's commemoration ceremonies every year since his passing. So I should have known where I was going.

But I have absolutely no sense of direction, and though I knew I was in the right vicinity, I could not find the grave. "I'm just disoriented because I've driven in. I know what I'll do," I thought. "I'll go back out the gates and walk through like I normally do. I won't think — I'll just go where my feet instinctively take me."

But it was no use. I couldn't find that tall, plain granite headstone that is Luke's marker. I stalked back and forth across the graves, trying to see in my mind's eye the gentle rise of the land where Luke is buried. And then I found it, the spot now covered by a strip of plywood. The flowers were all gone, piled into the waste bin at the front of the cemetery. Then, a truly shocking thought began to dawn. "The headstone is gone. Oh my God, Jimmy Kelly must have had it removed to re-inscribe it. And nobody has bothered to ask me what it should say." I was completely demented, beside myself with anger and rage.

"How dare they," I fumed, calling down every possible curse and damnation on the unfortunate Jimmy — Luke's brother — and even on my complicit brother, Emmett. "Typical males," I raged. "Think they know it all. Take charge. Get the business done. No thought given to how anyone else feels." I leapt into my car and tore home. And I began making furious telephone calls around the country. But nobody was home.

What followed was a morning of sheer madness. I located a photograph of Deirdre, encased it within two panes of glass and wrapped it in sheets of plastic to shield it against the rain. Then I planted up an assortment of evergreens and headed back to the cemetery with my handmade monument.

I quickly found the unmarked grave and laid out my memorial. It would have to do until I could get this sorted out.

I finally got a bewildered Emmett on the phone the next day. "Hey, calm down, Gerry," he said. "What's all the hysteria about?

Maybe Jimmy did remove the headstone but I'm sure he only wants to do the right thing. Tell me what you want on it and I'll get in touch with Jimmy."

We agreed on a very simple inscription:

> "Deirdre O'Connell
> 1939–2001
> Founder of Focus Theatre"

Relieved that all was in safe hands, I went about my life, and another fortnight later, on my way home from Belfast with Kaniah, I decided to drop in for a chat with Deirdre.

Once again, I drove through the gates, leaving Kaniah in the car, and headed straight for the grave. And once again, I was lost. It looked like a plague of some sort had hit Dublin, what with acres of open graves gaping all around me. Was I losing the grip, or what?

Kaniah was watching quietly from the car, and noticing my frenzied state, got out and headed off past me. "You're going in the wrong direction," I called, full sure that I knew the right spot. And then I heard her call in the distance, "Hey, Mom, come on over here." As I looked over towards the railroad tracks, I could see the familiar granite stone.

"Nothing's been done to it, Mom. I thought you said it was meant to be re-inscribed."

"Oh Jesus Christ!" I flew back to my original spot and then I found it. The plywood slab and now, a very faded and drenched-looking photograph of Deirdre sitting on the wrong grave.

Emmett fell around the place laughing when, next day, I beat my breast and apologised profusely for my wicked thoughts. "Can you just picture some poor unfortunate woman, going out to visit her newly departed husband, and finding this strange woman's photograph sitting on top of it. Oh Gerry, what have you done?"

"What have I done?" I moaned. "There she is. Deirdre. Six feet under and still stirring things up."

⍒

DEIRDRE HAD MADE HER CHOICES and she never looked back. But the choices have not been that clear for many others. Divided loyalties continue to tow and tug and in these stormy days of global conflict, uncertain identities become more troubling than ever. Choices must be made and loyalties declared.

As Britain fades into the background of Irish political life, the European Union takes centre-stage. The question can no longer be "Am I Irish or am I American?" The question is now, "Am I Irish, or am I American, or am I neither of these? Am I European?" Furthermore, for those who never left Ireland's shores, the dilemma will now be the same. Where will their loyalties lie? Will old historical ties across the Atlantic hold in the face of new political realities? In short, will it be the Bronx or Brussels, San Francisco or Strasbourg, Boston or Berlin?

Children of the Far-Flung bequeath their struggle to you.

⍒